Cat Mandalas Adult Coloring Book Vol 4

60 Entertaining Stress Relieving Cat Patterns

By Omar Johnson

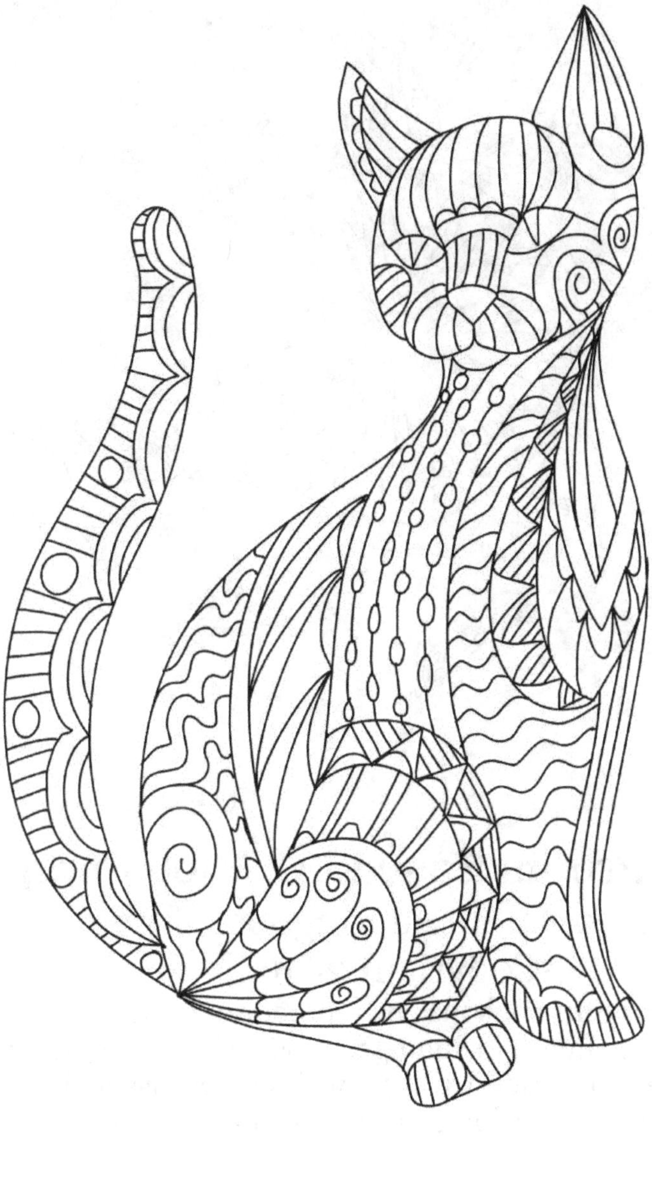

Get Your Free Butterfly Mandala Coloring Book

Visit

HTTPS://WWW.ADULTCOLORINGBOOKSFORYOU.COM

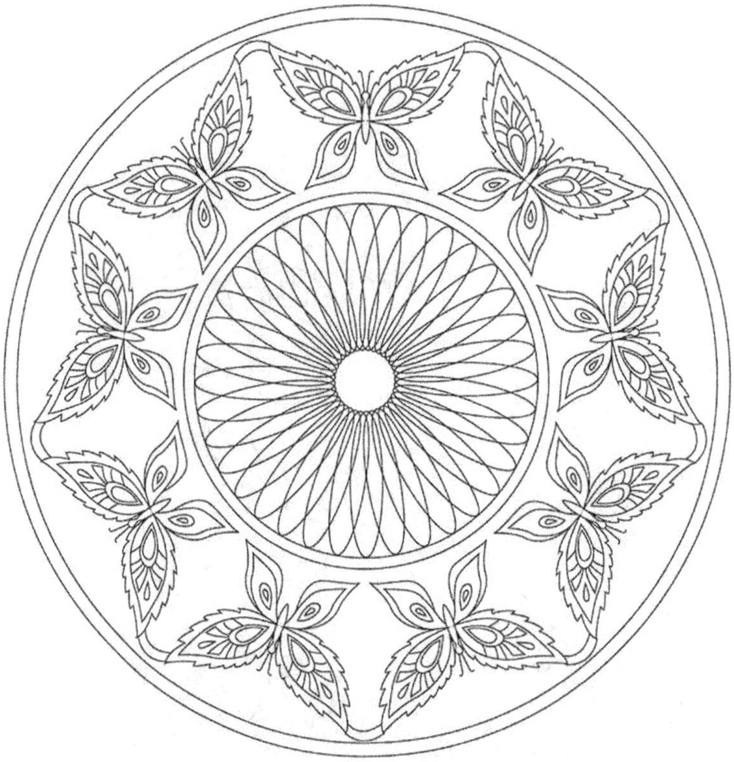

Make Profits Easy LLC Publishing

omarjohnson@adultcoloringbooksforyou.com

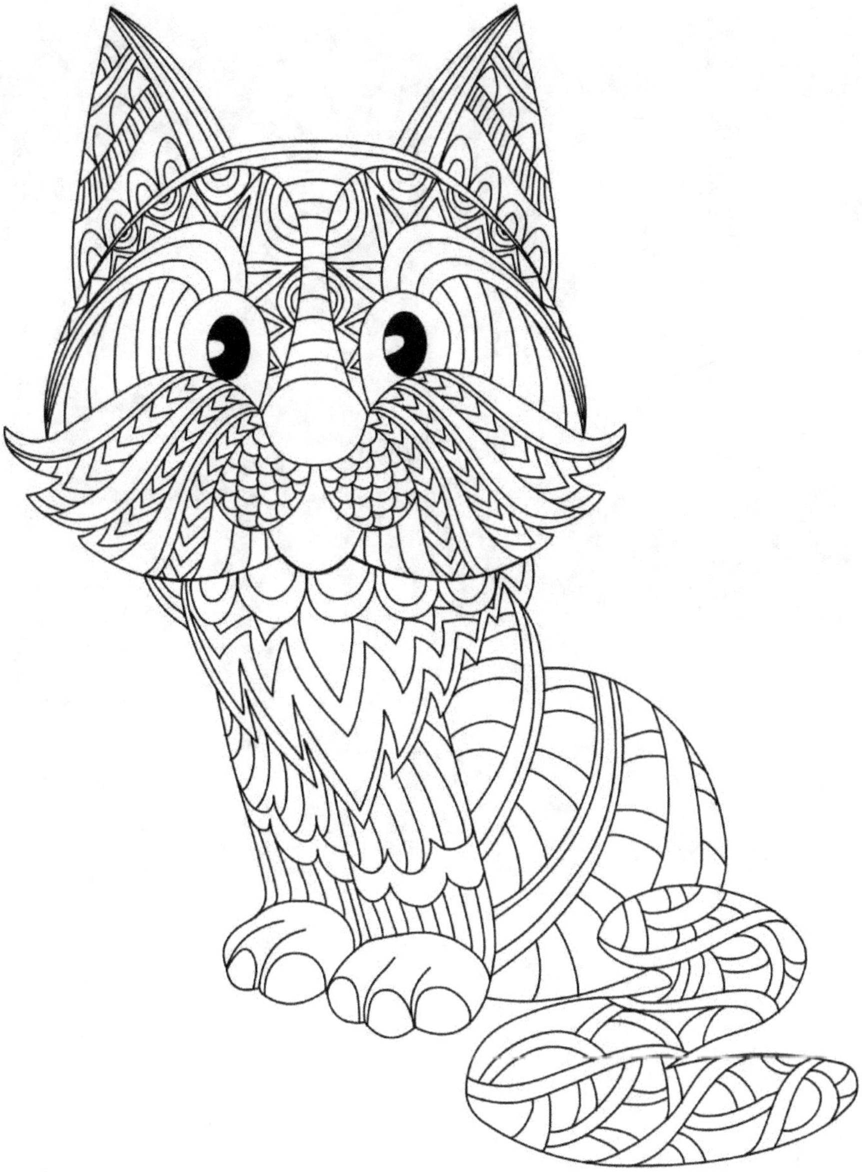

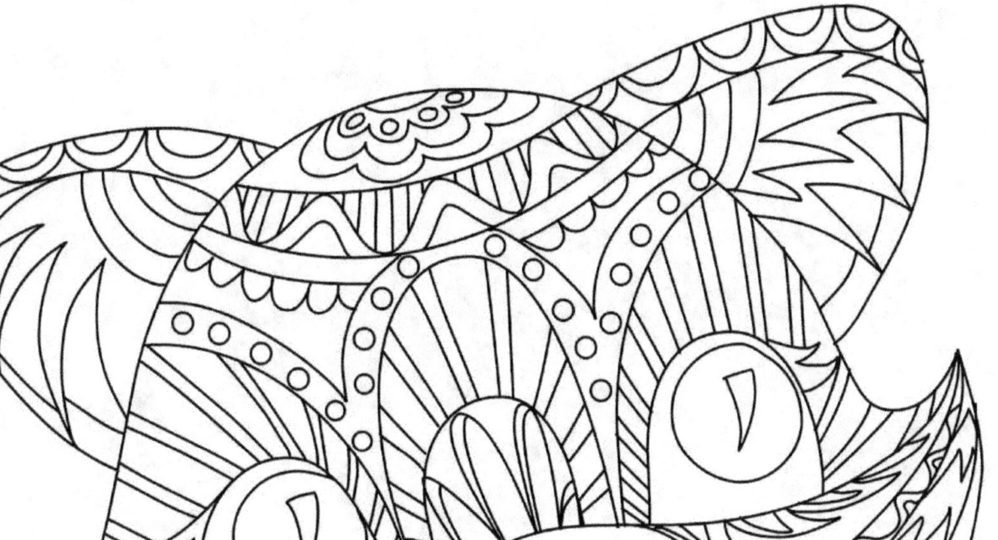

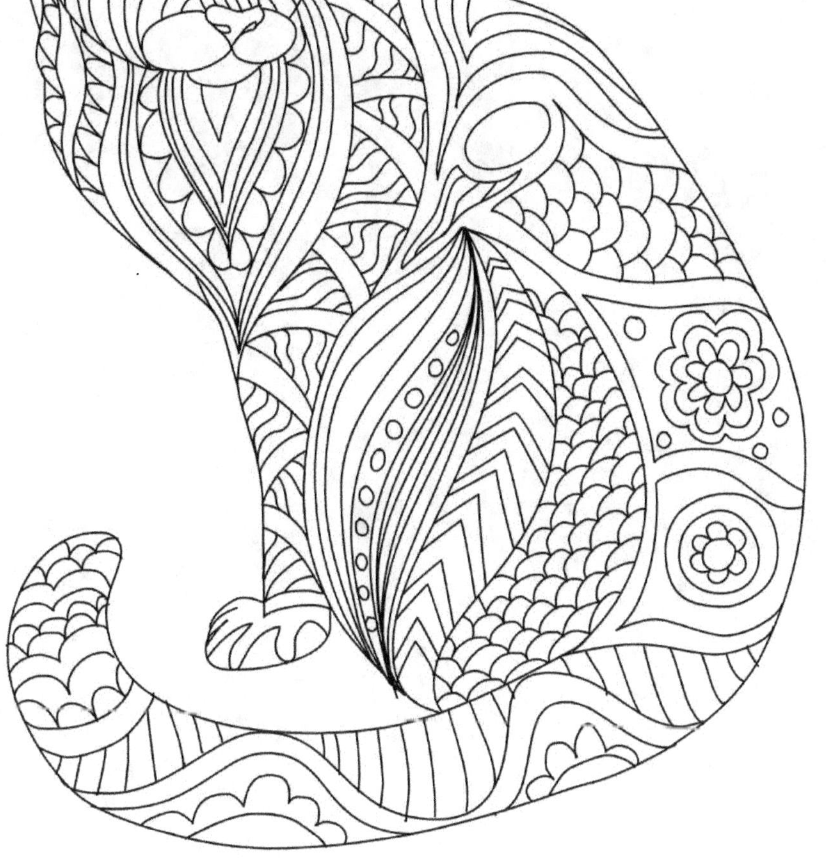

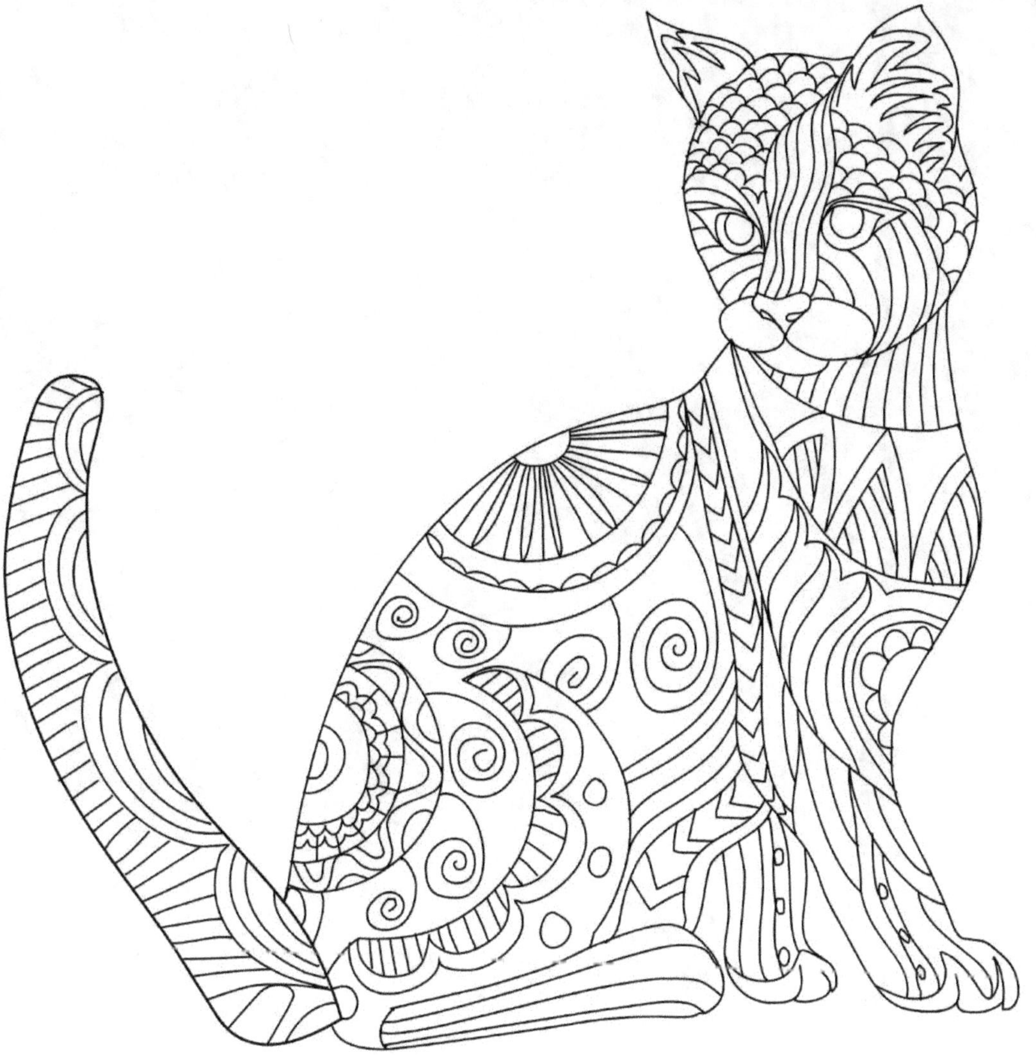

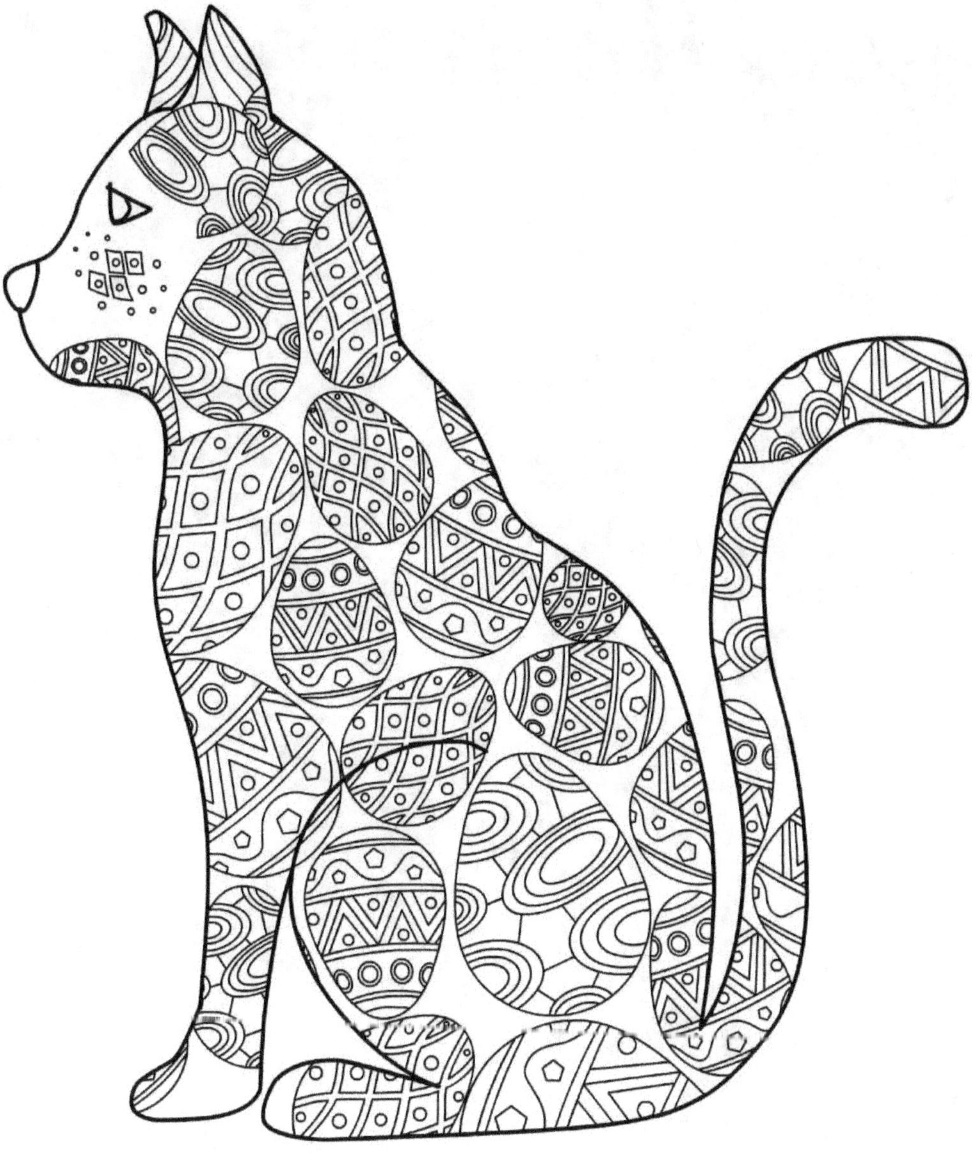

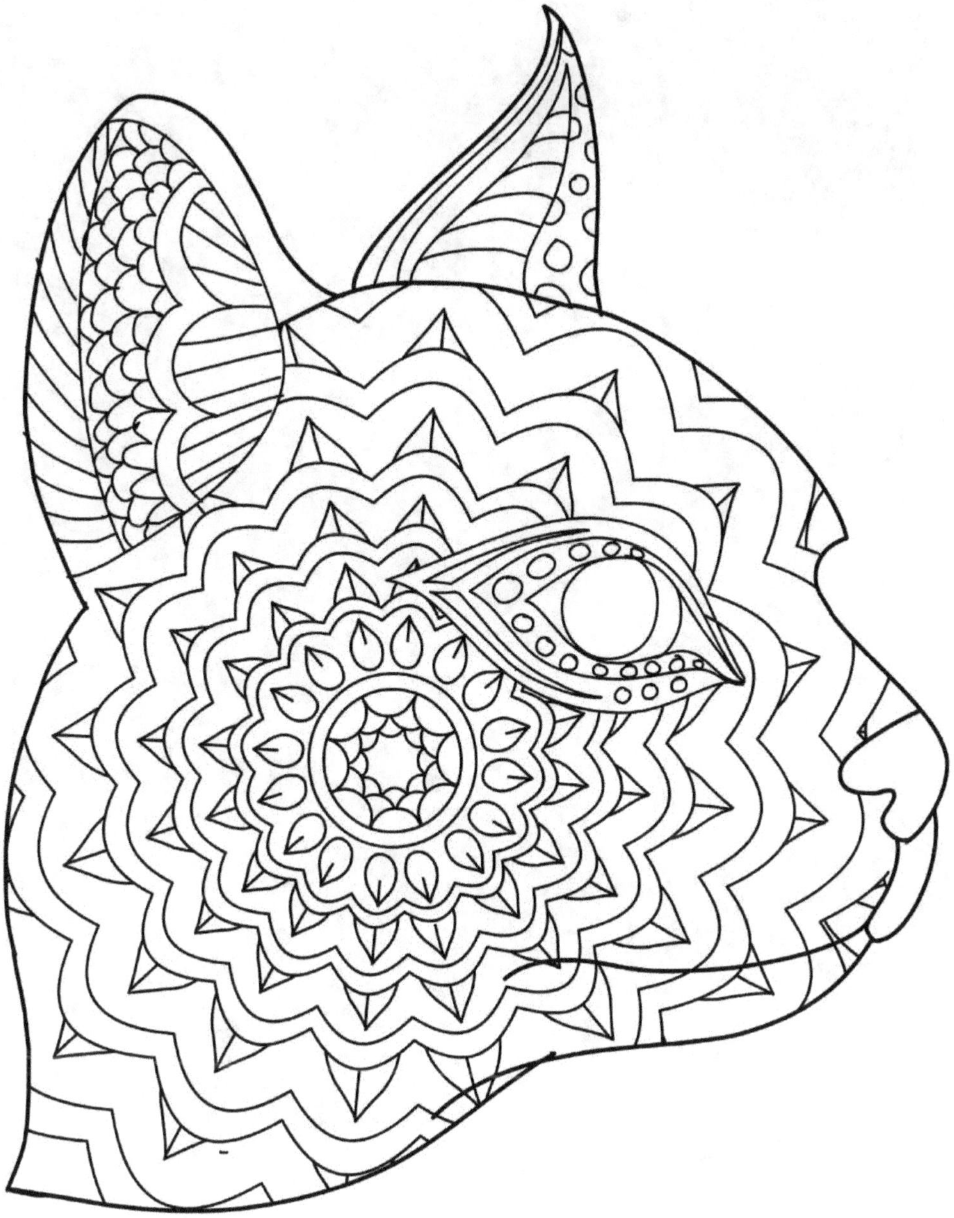

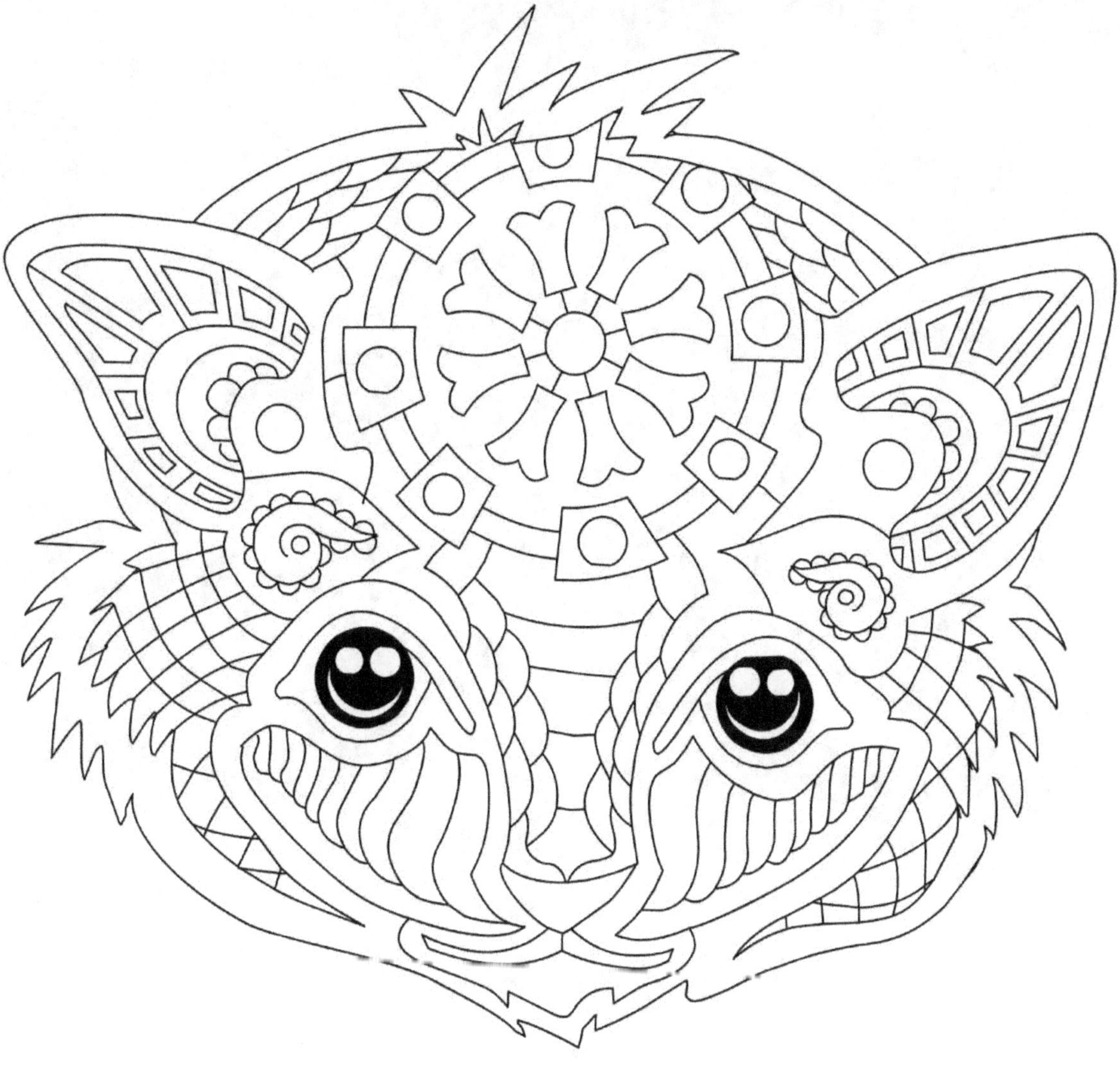

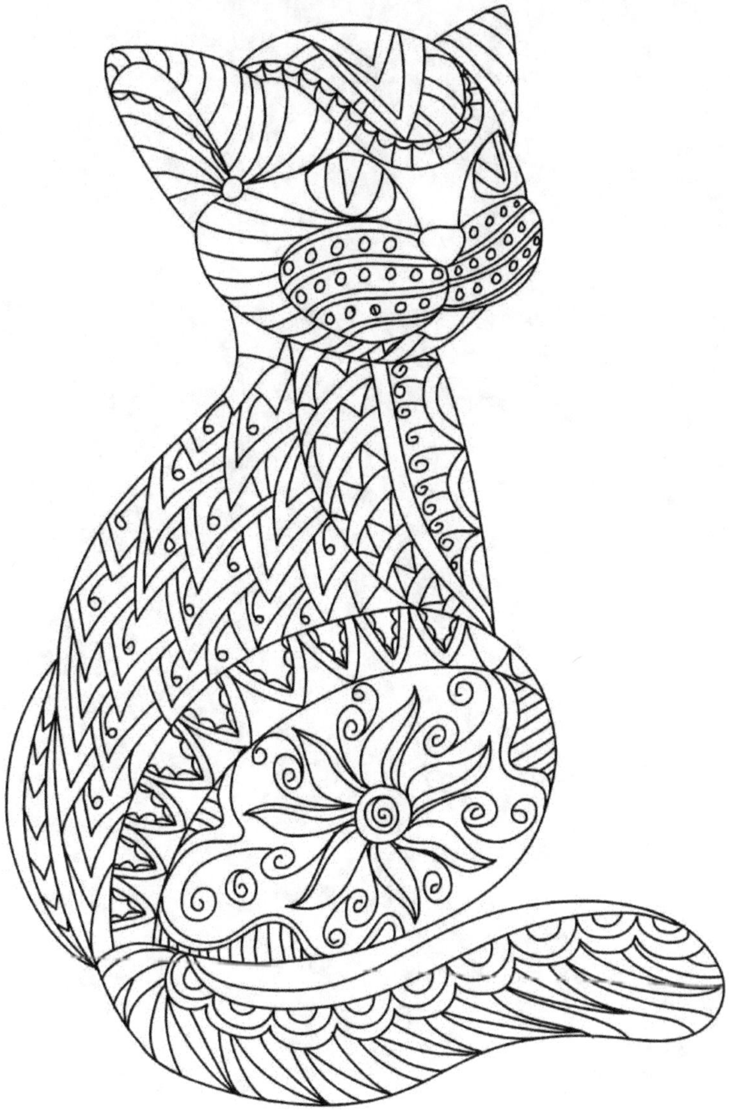

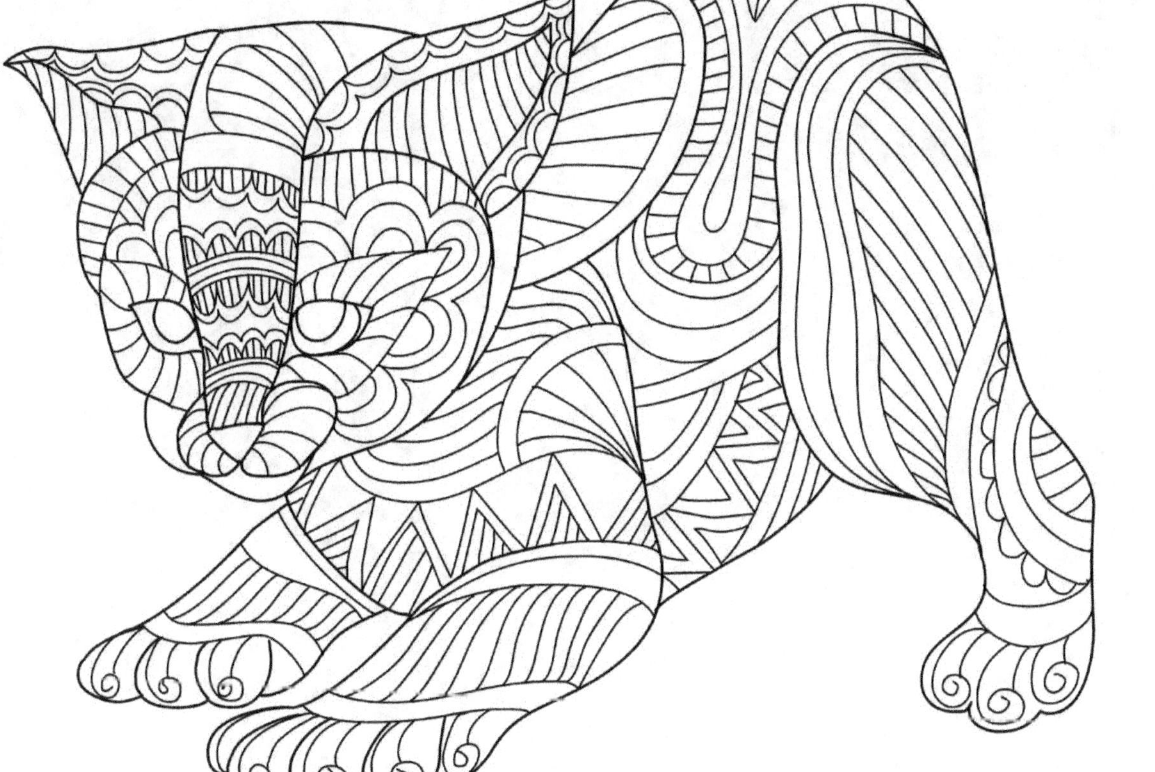

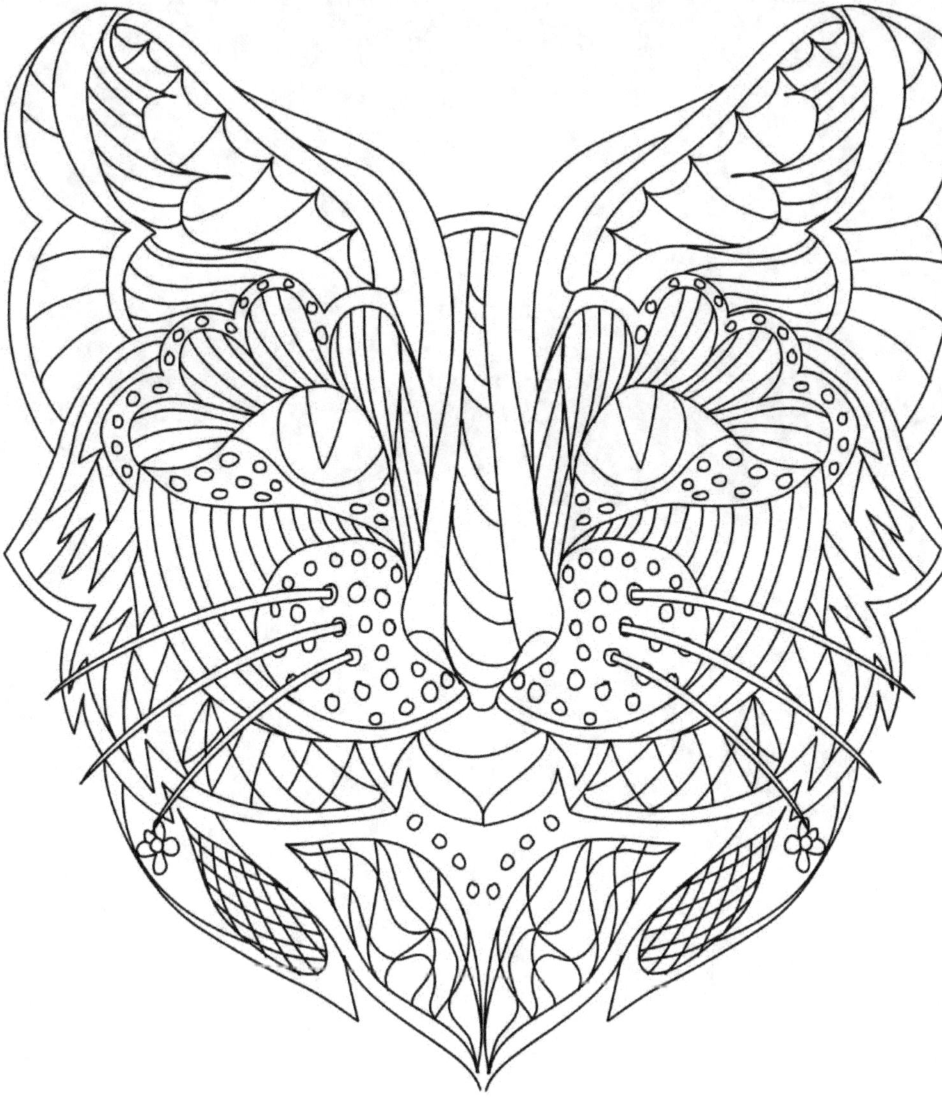

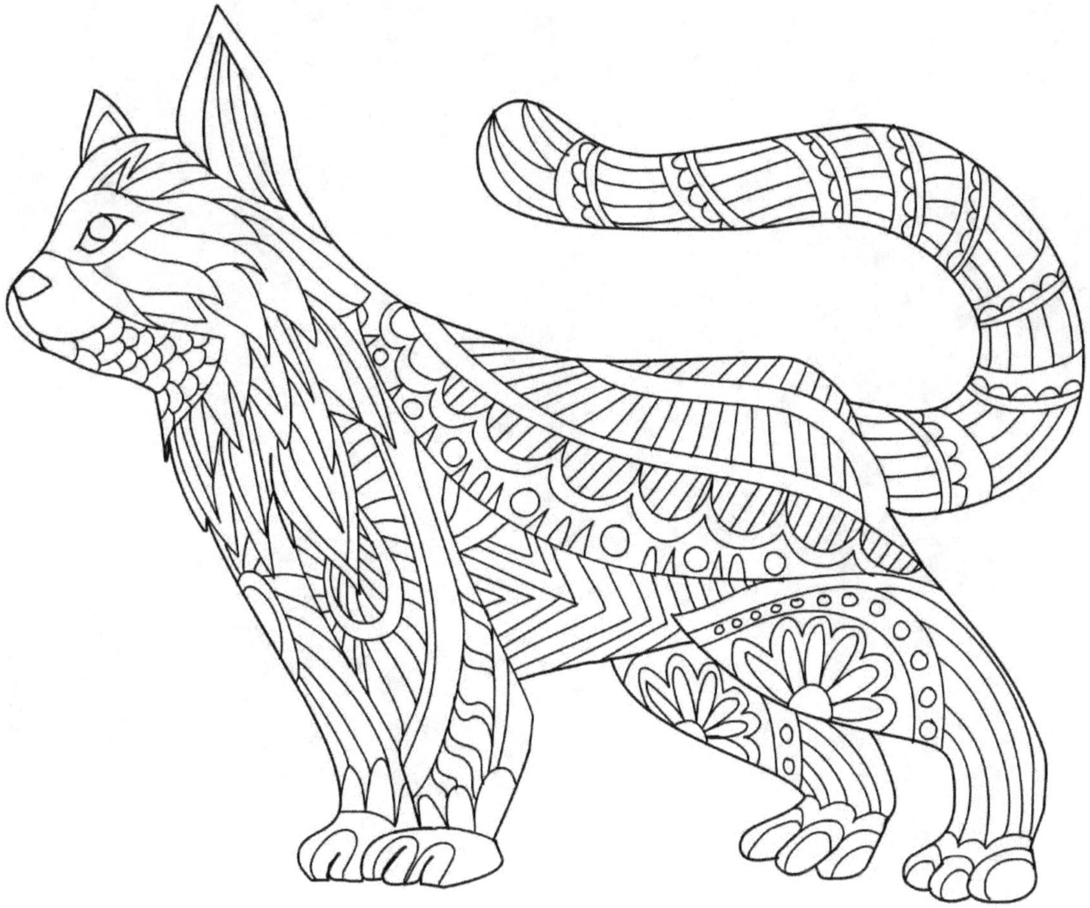

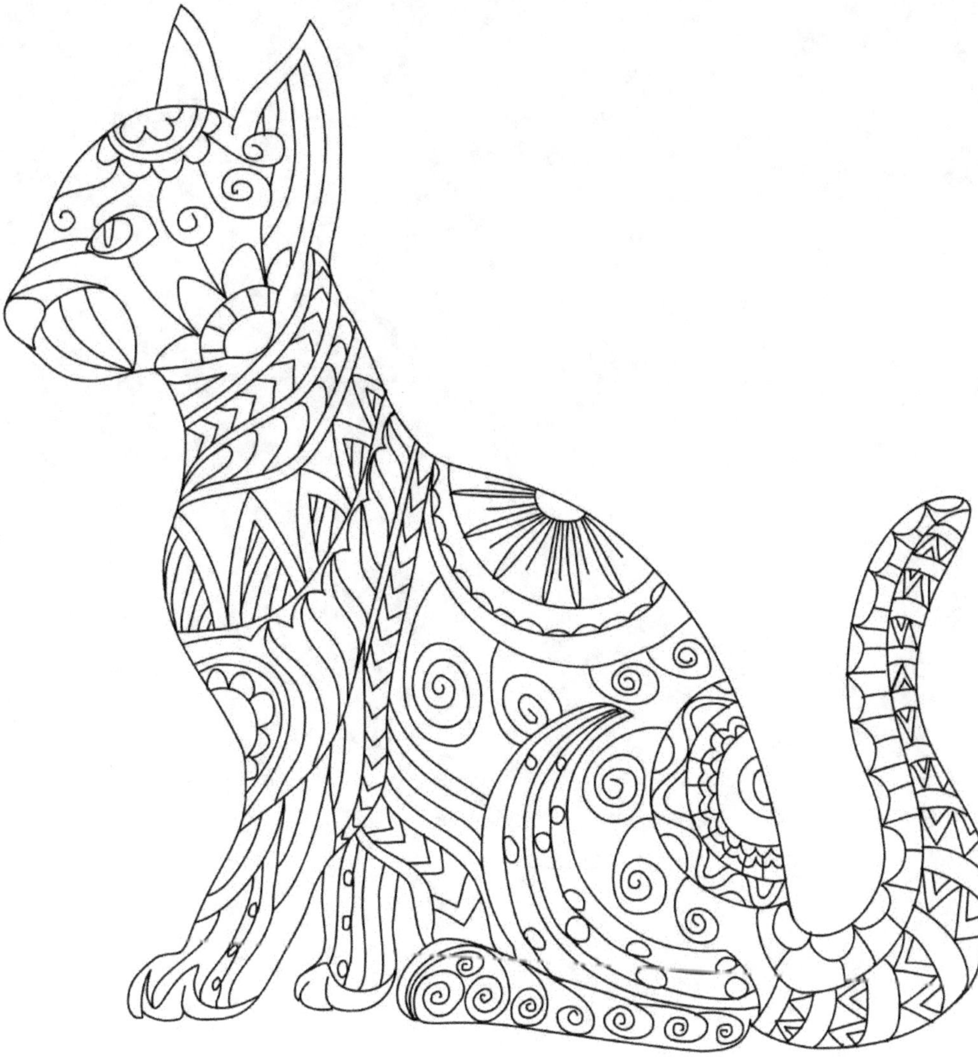

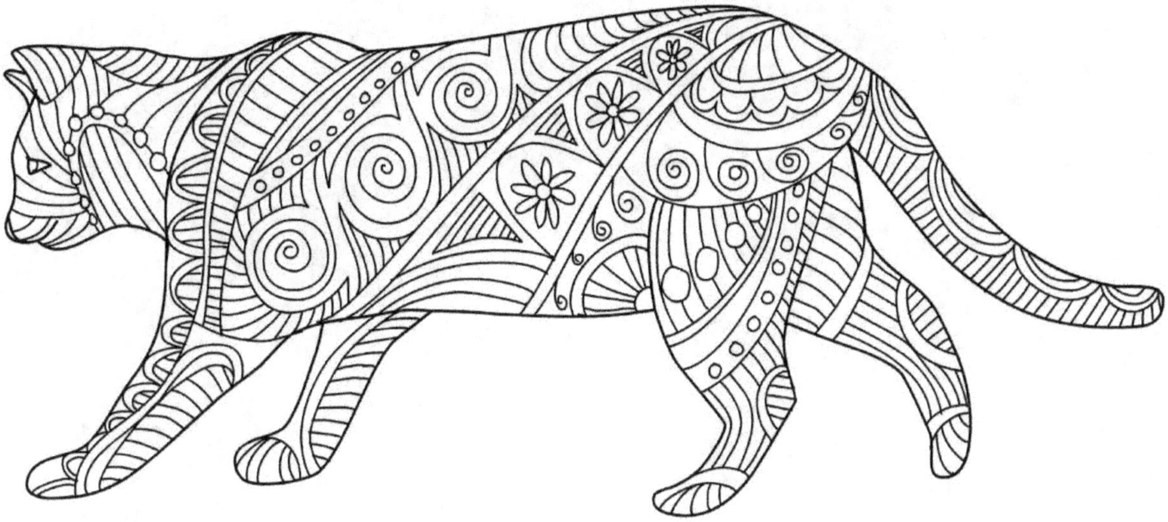

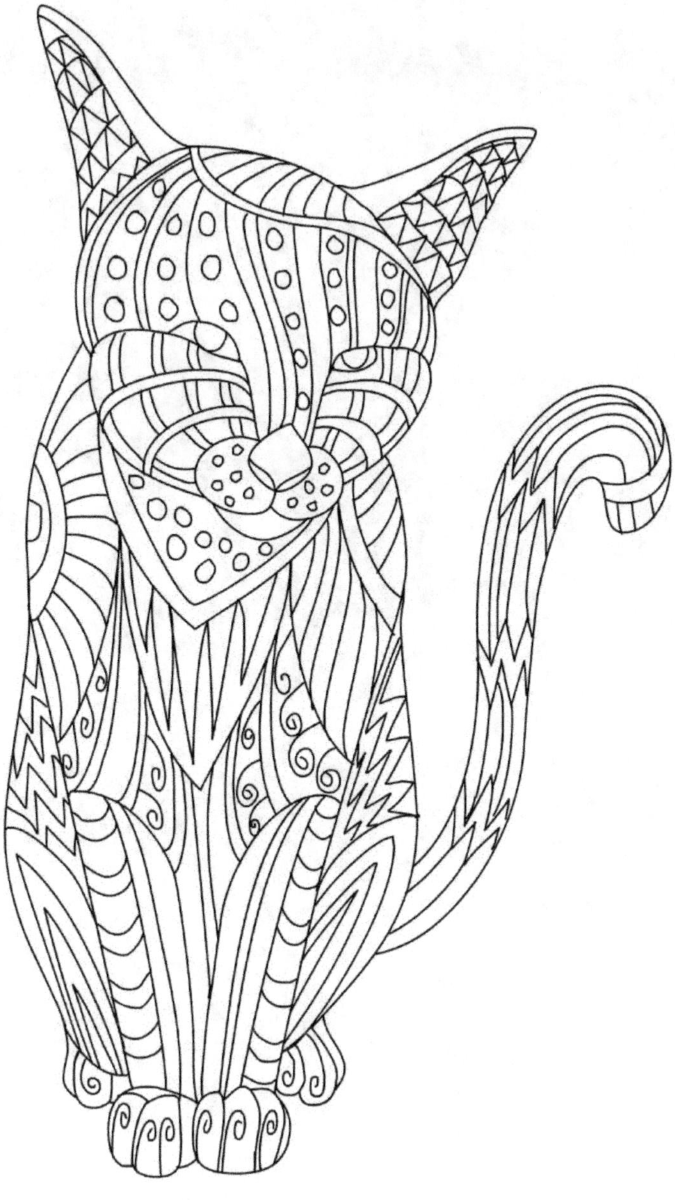

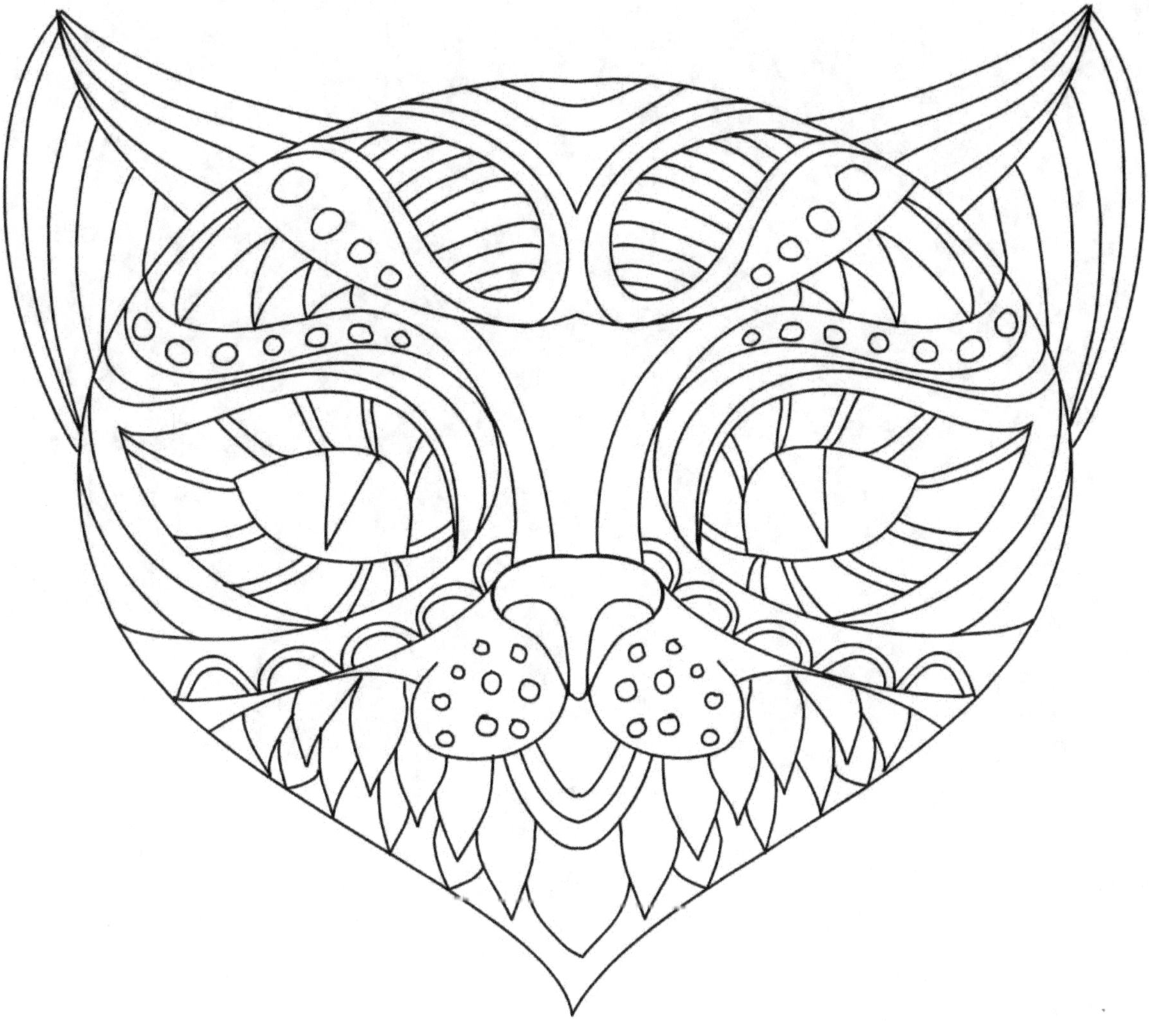

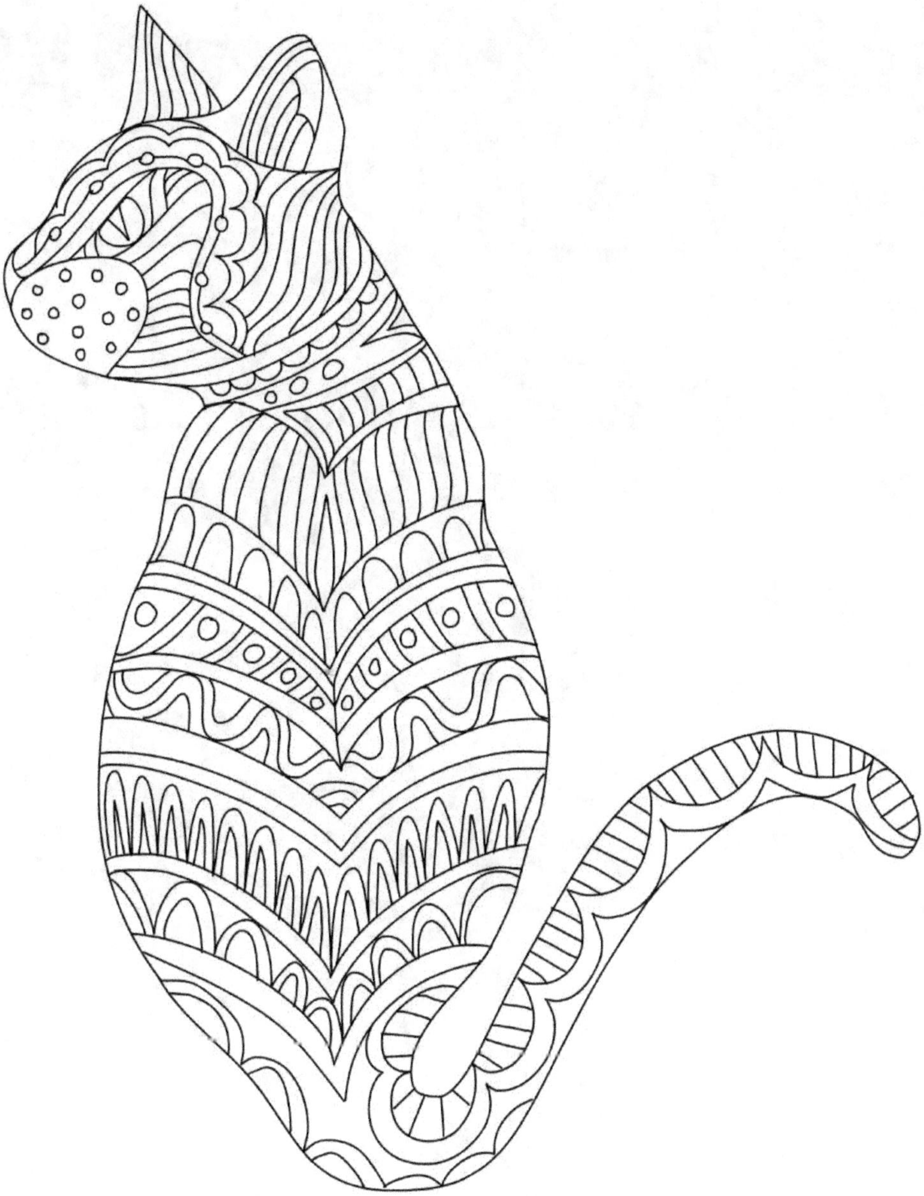

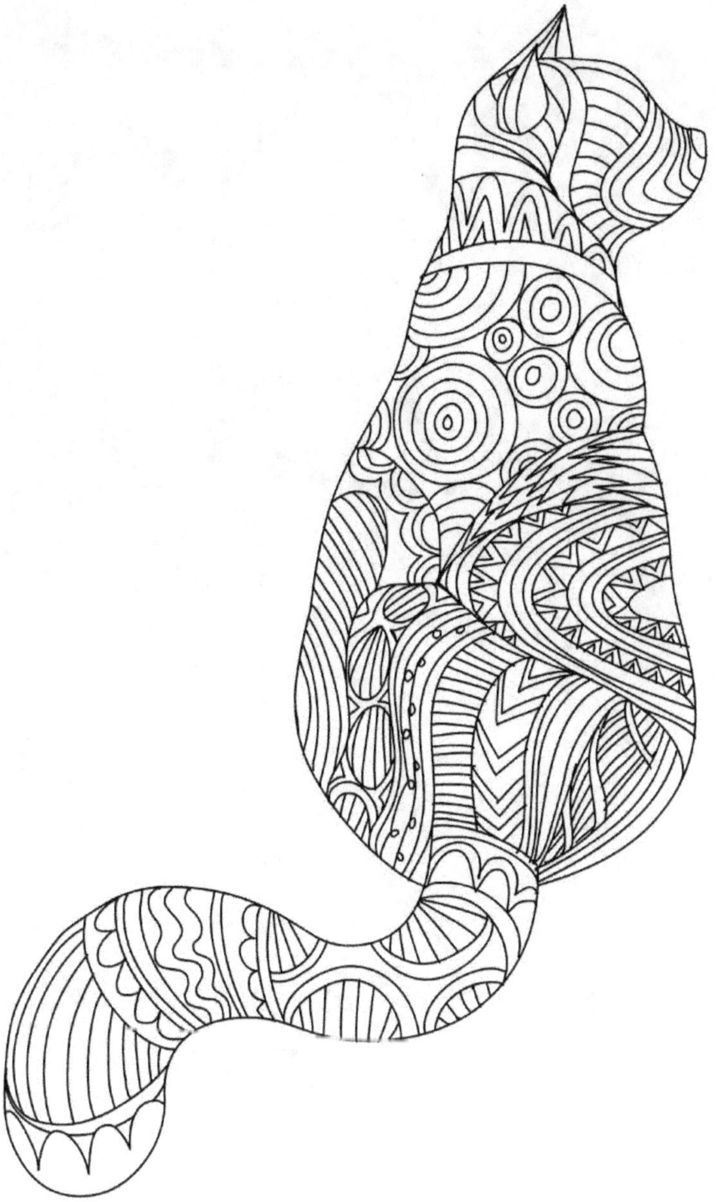

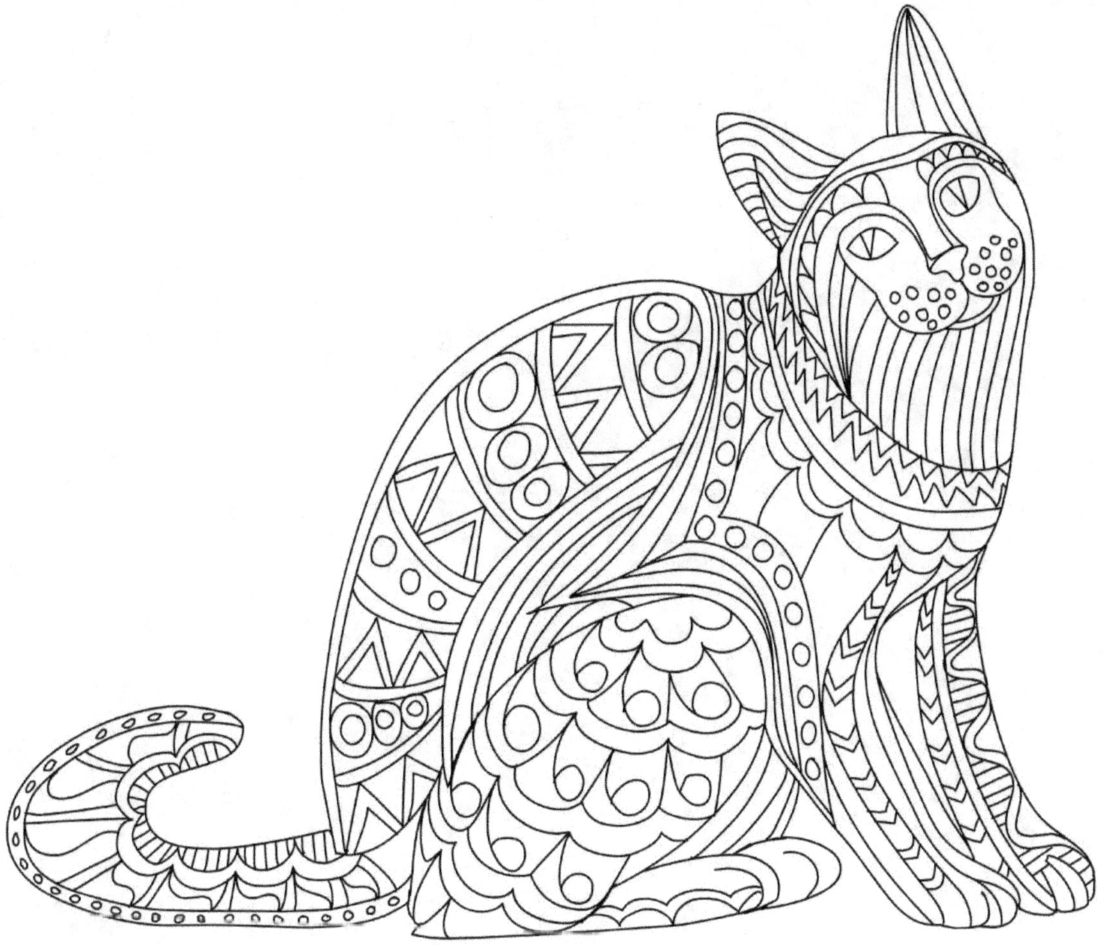

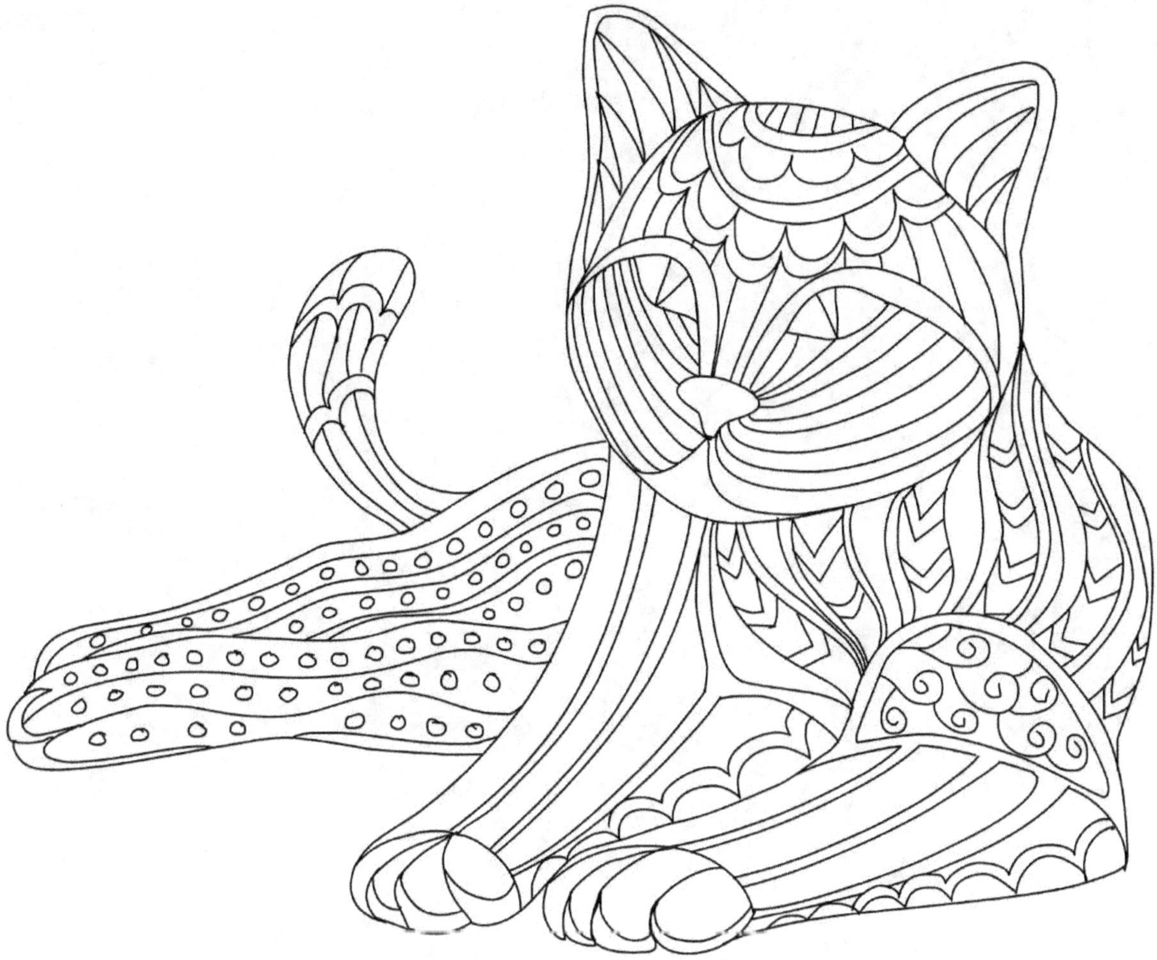

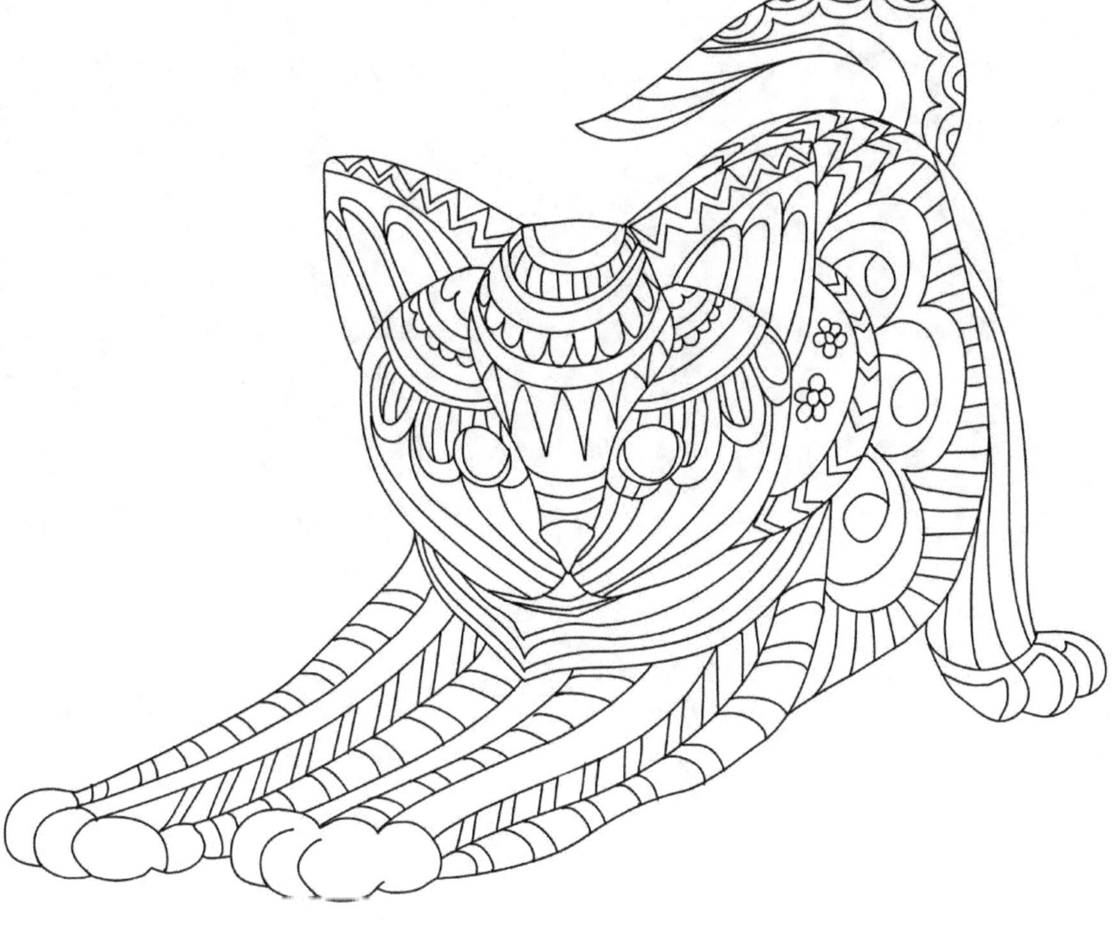

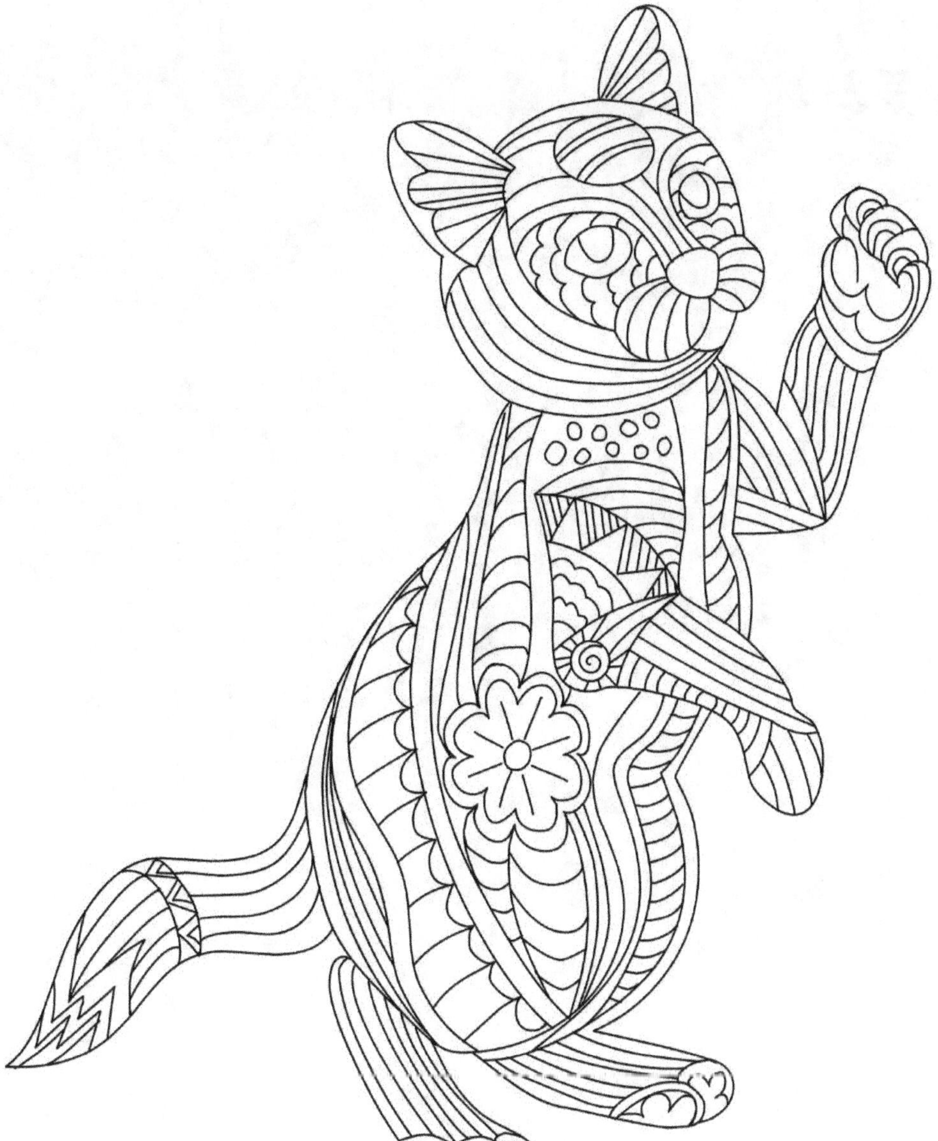

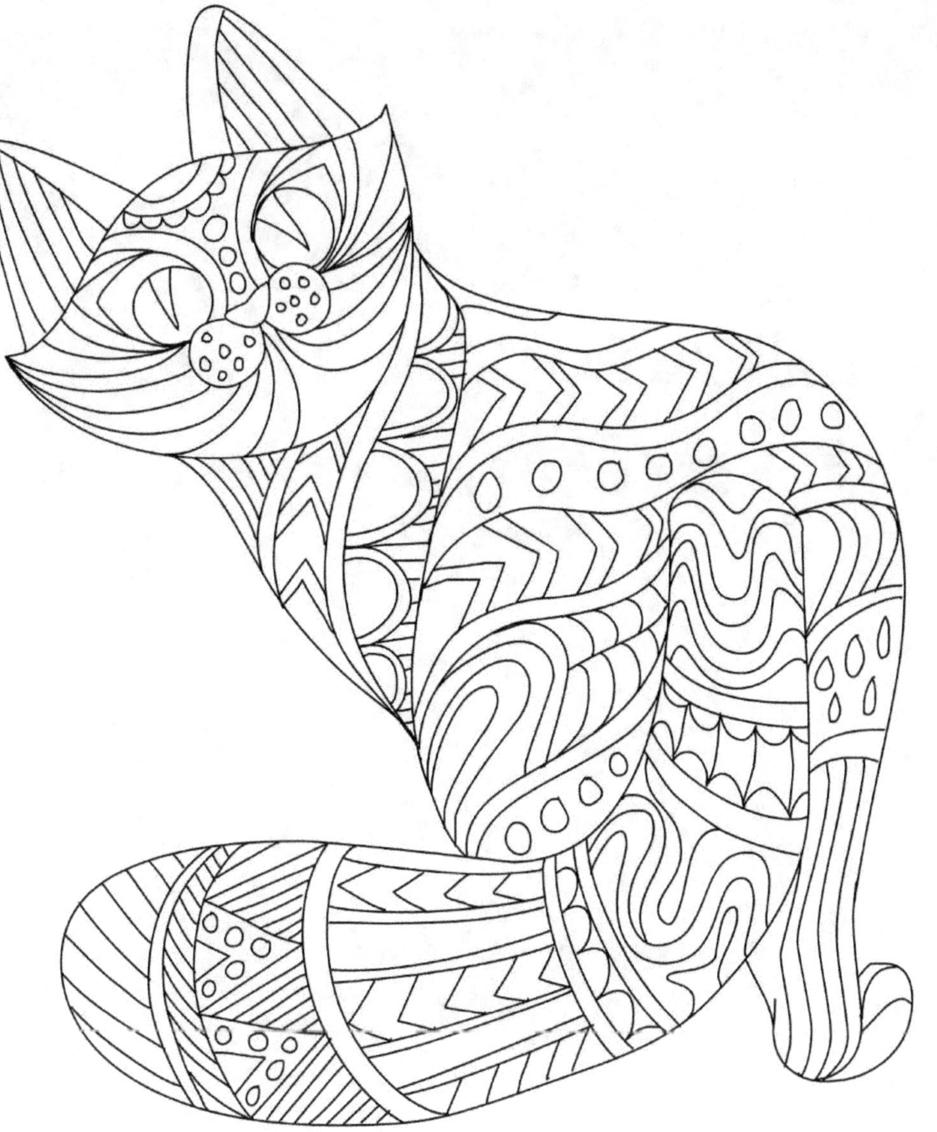

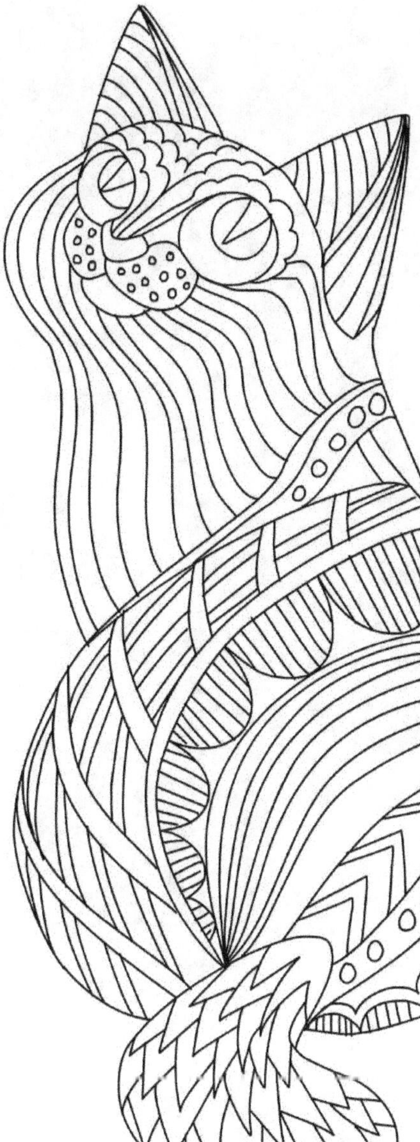

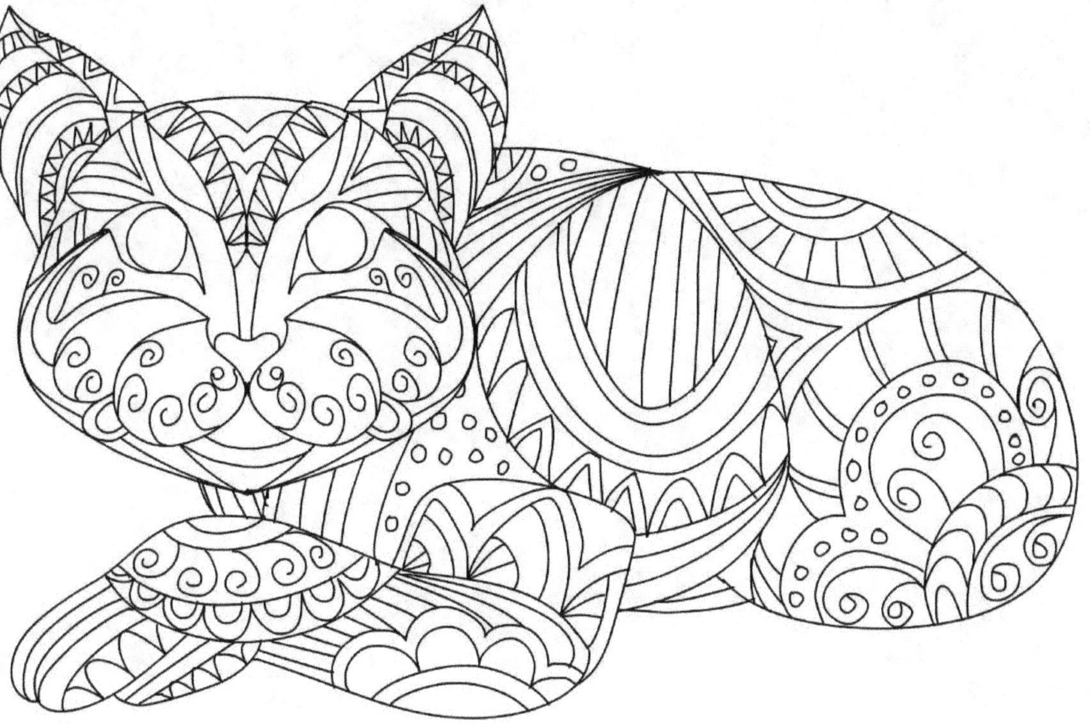

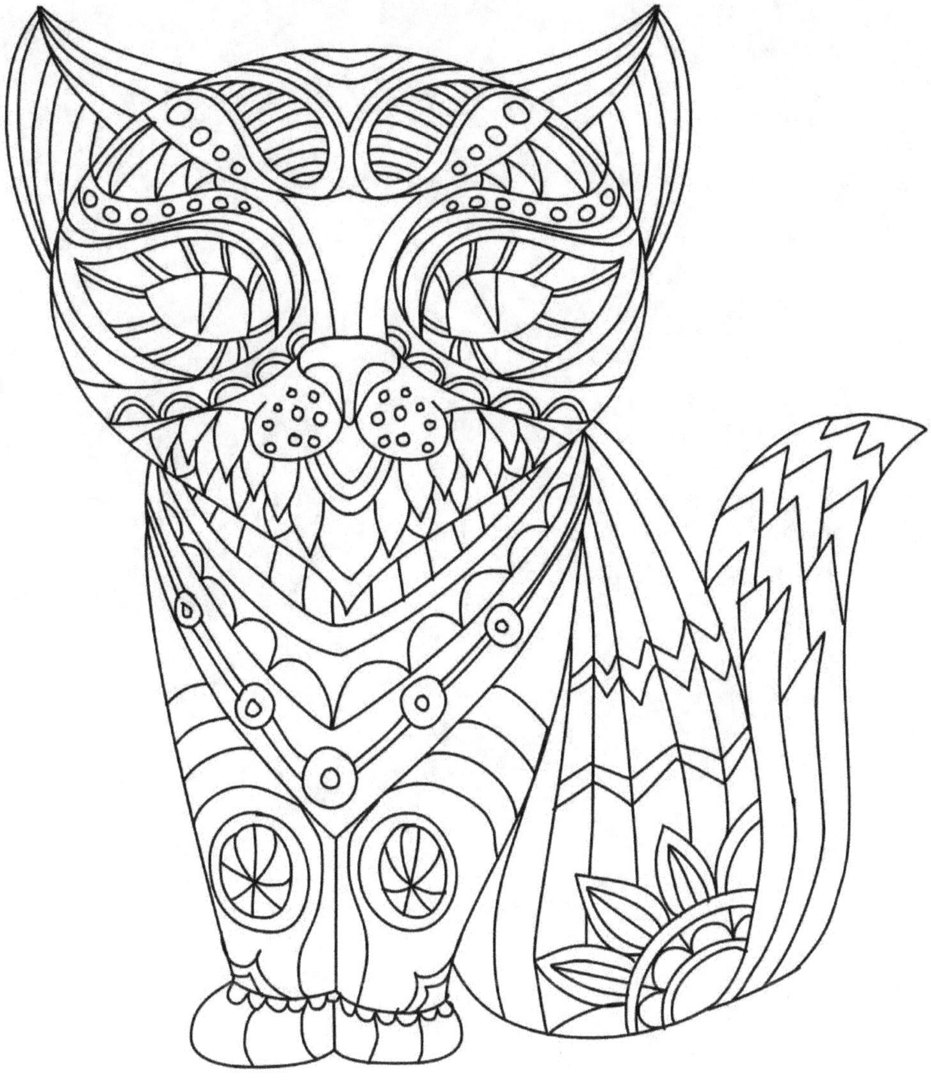

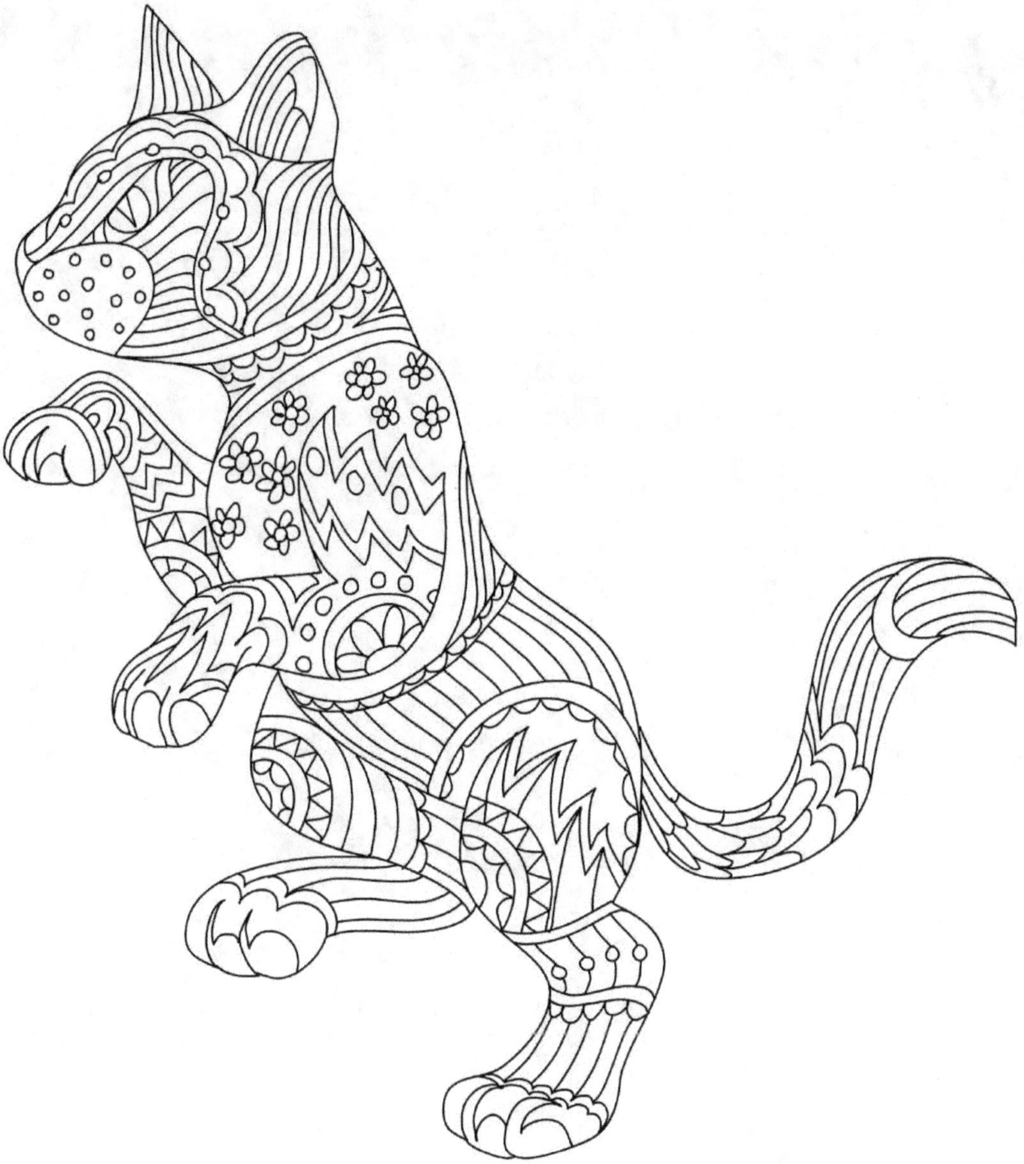

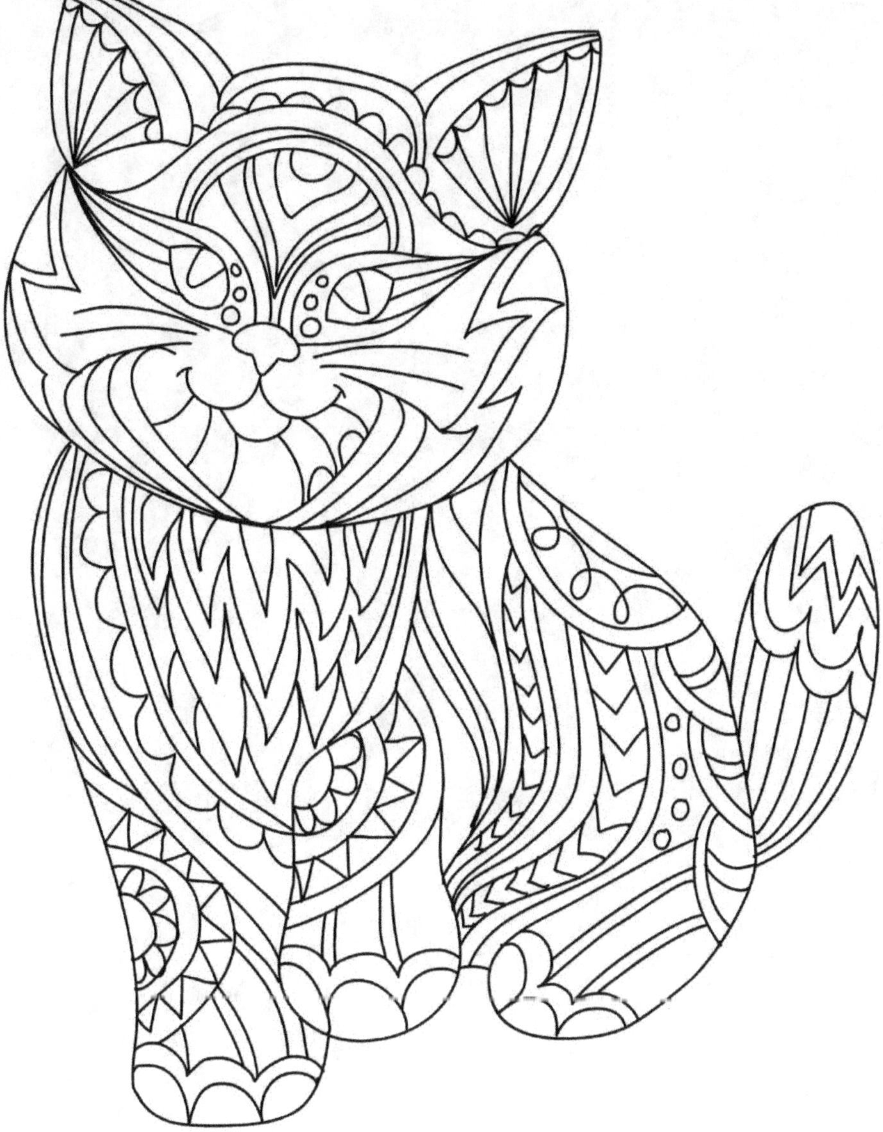

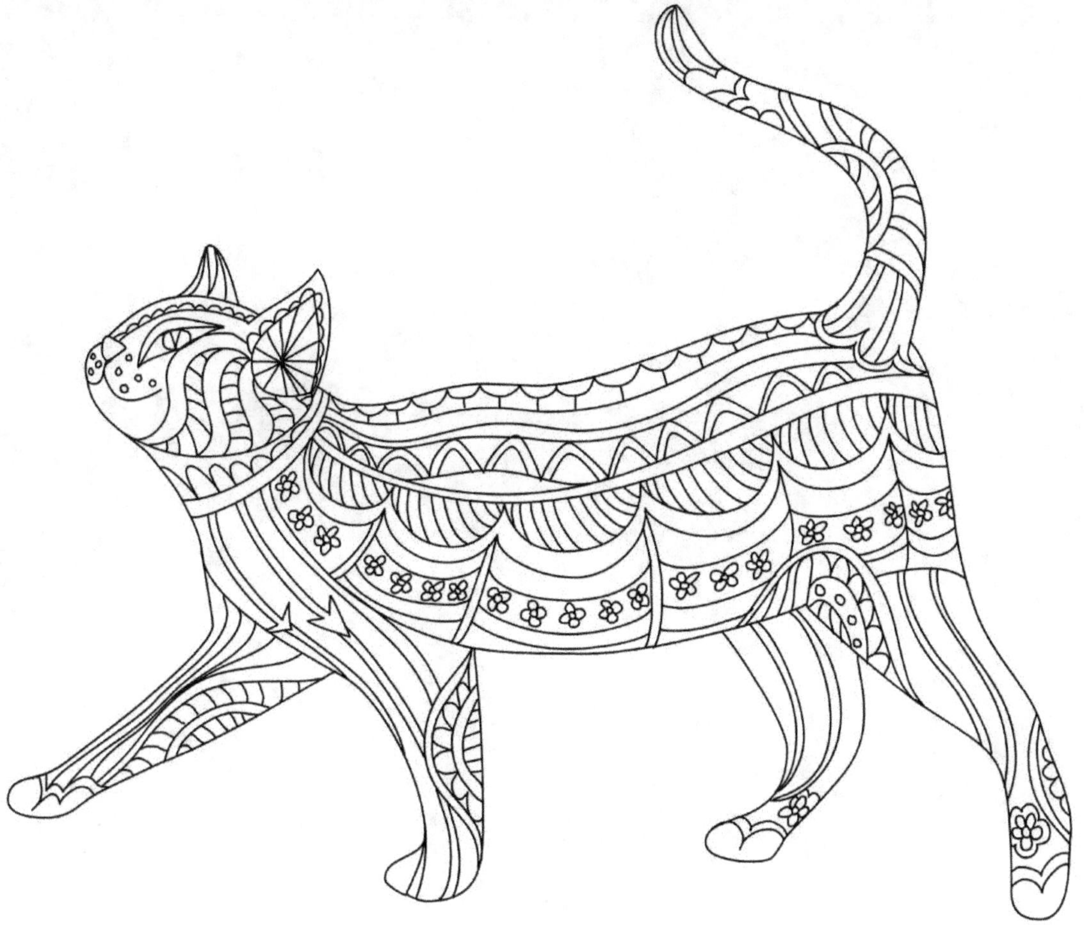

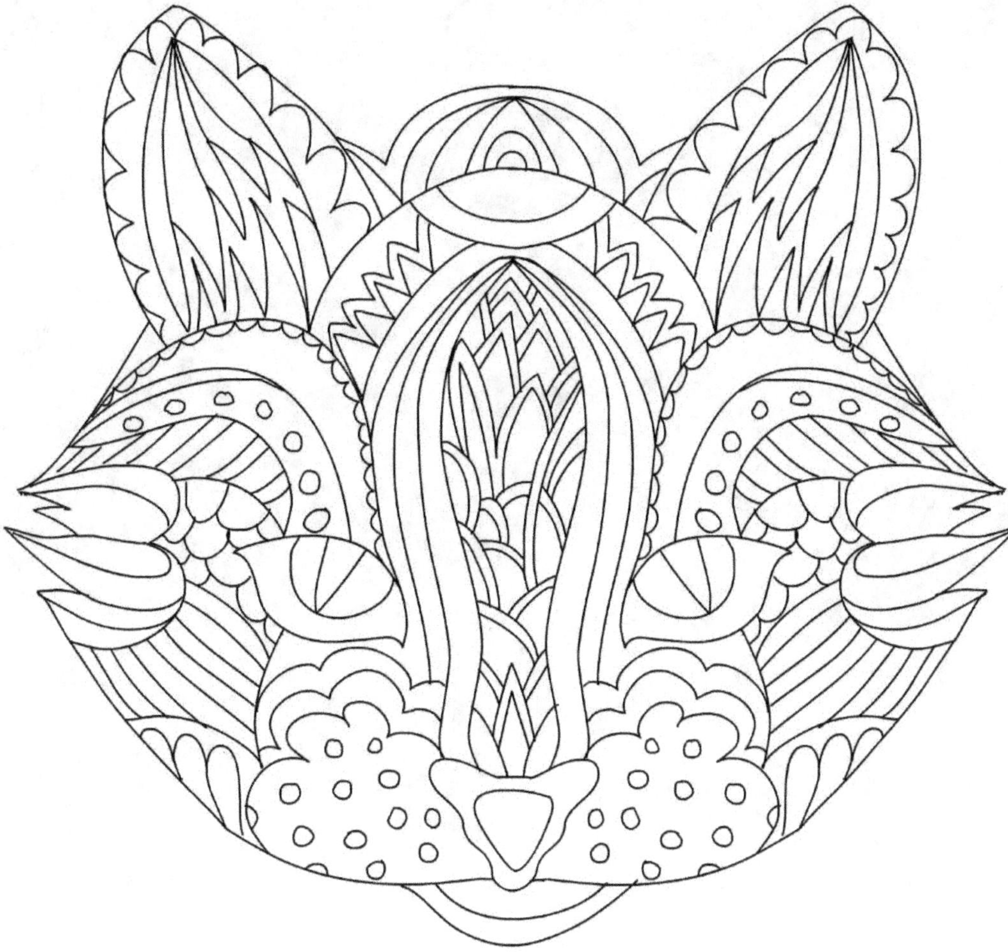

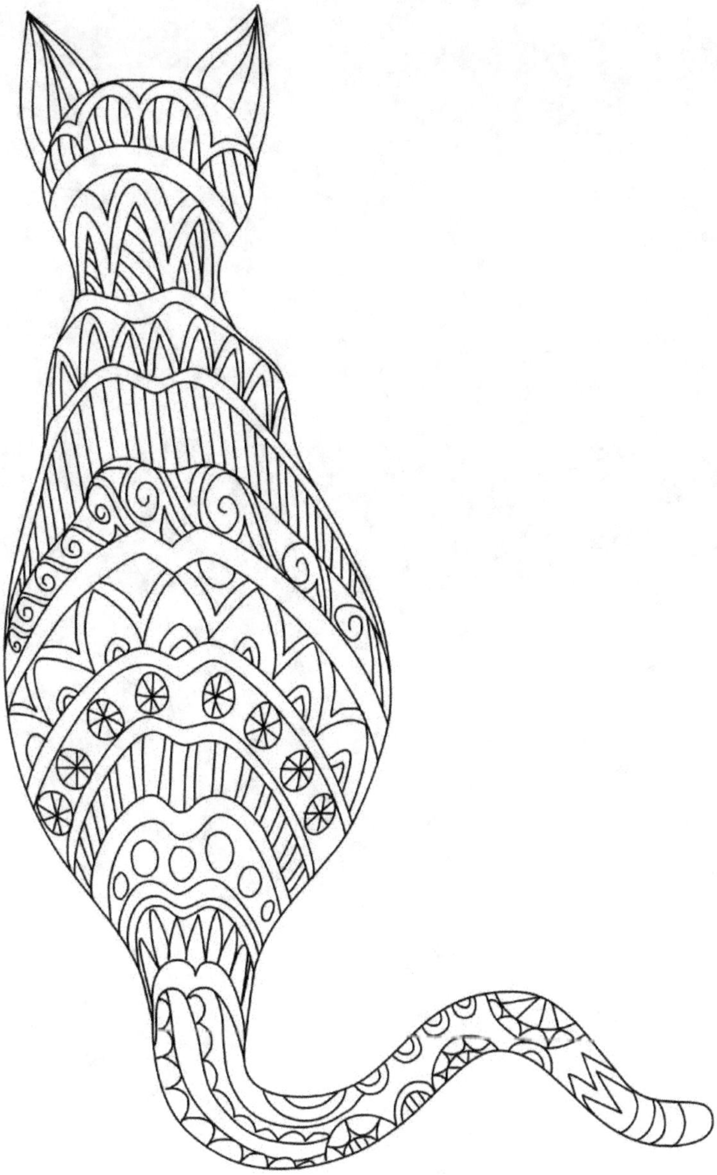

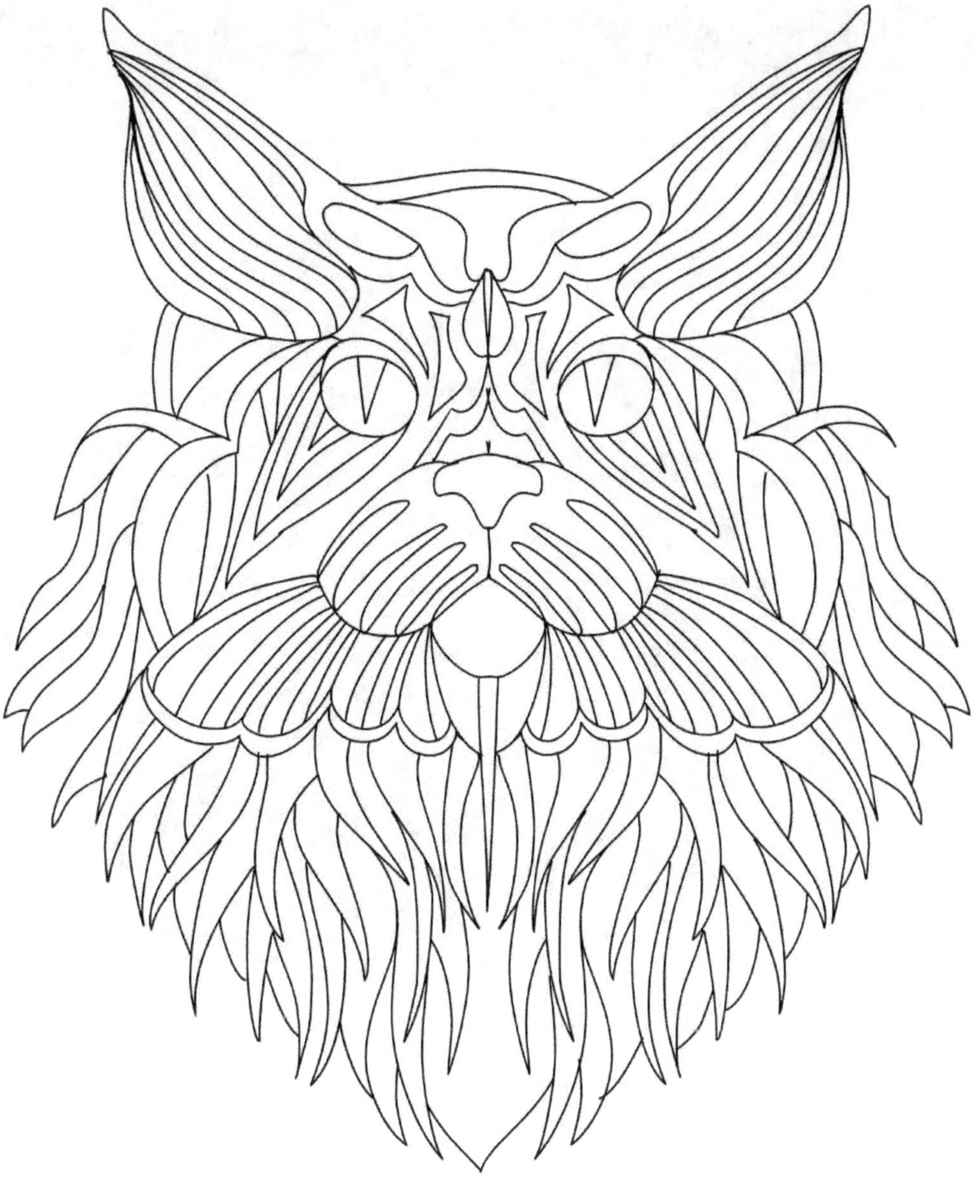

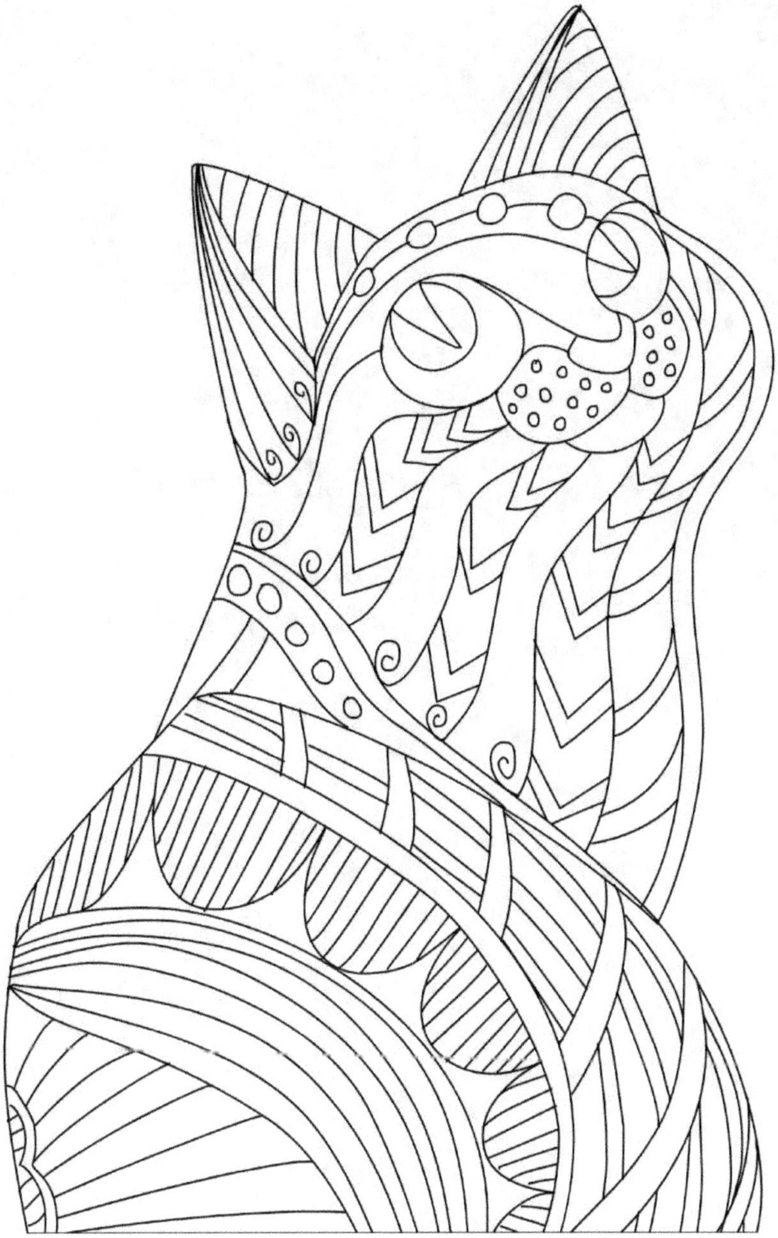

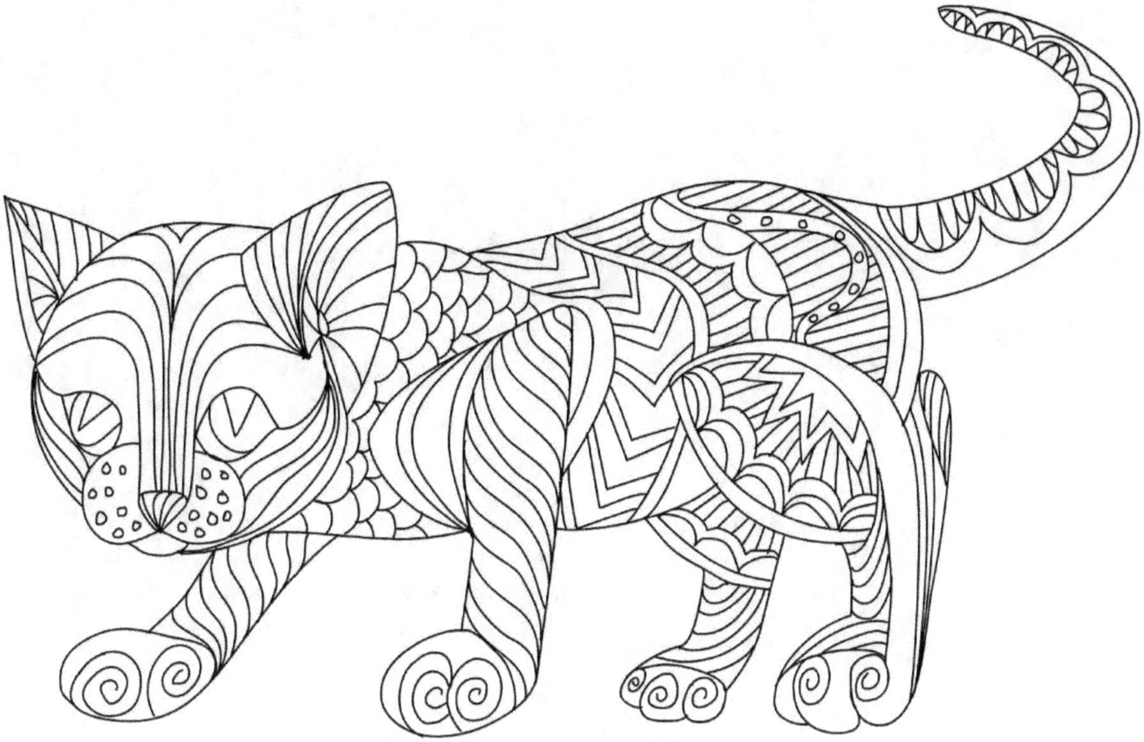

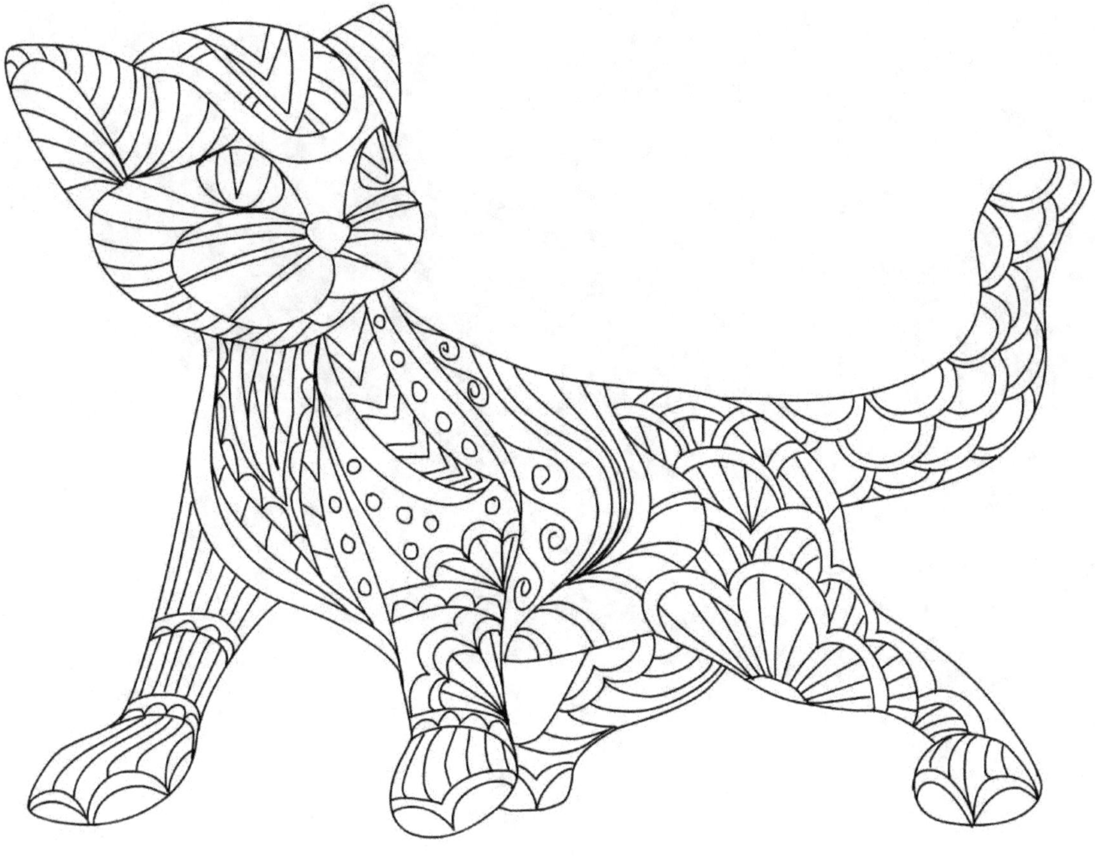

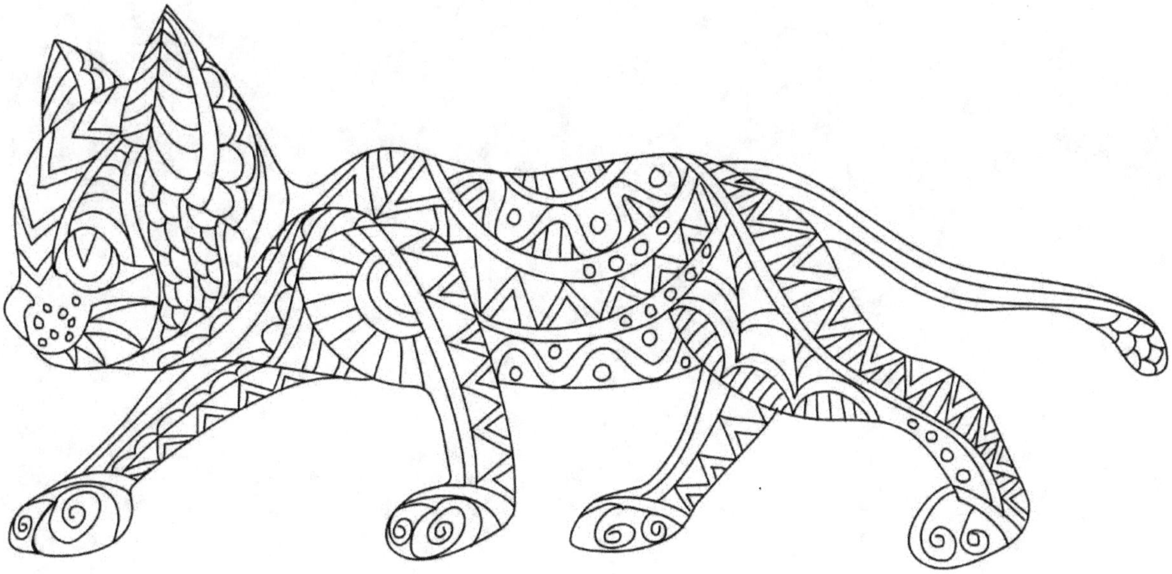

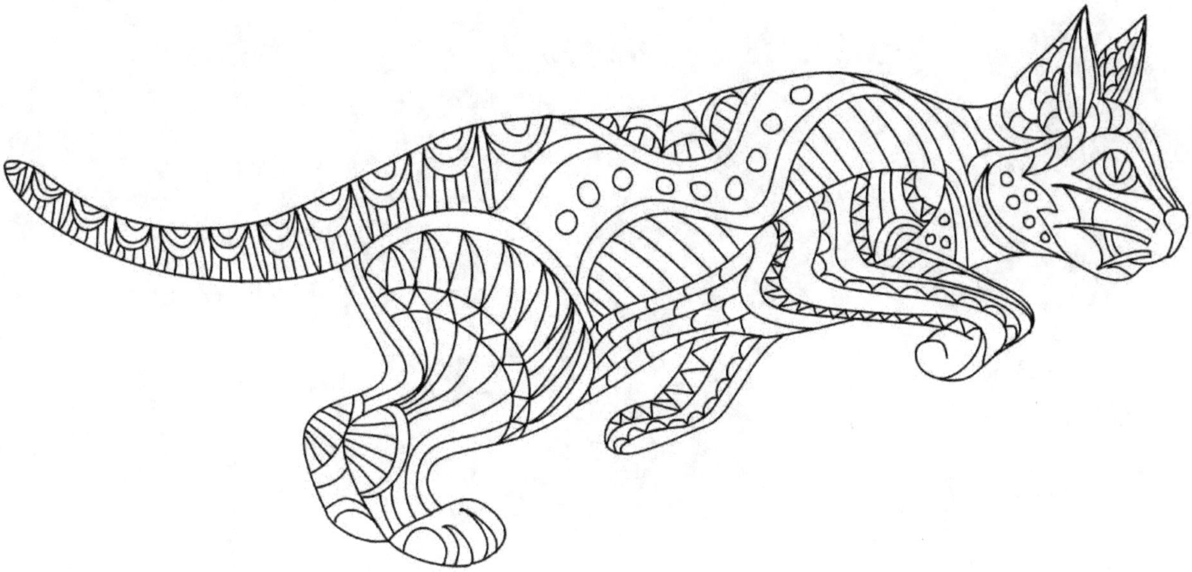

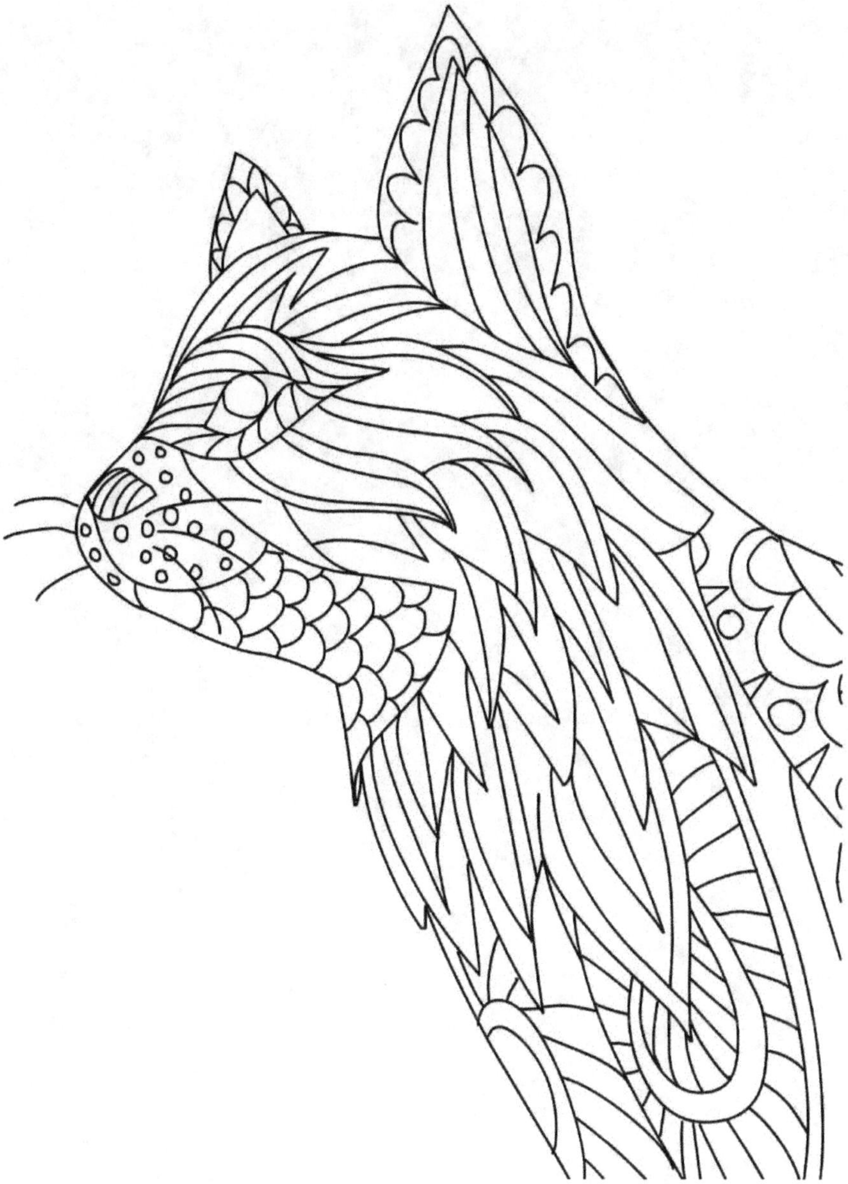

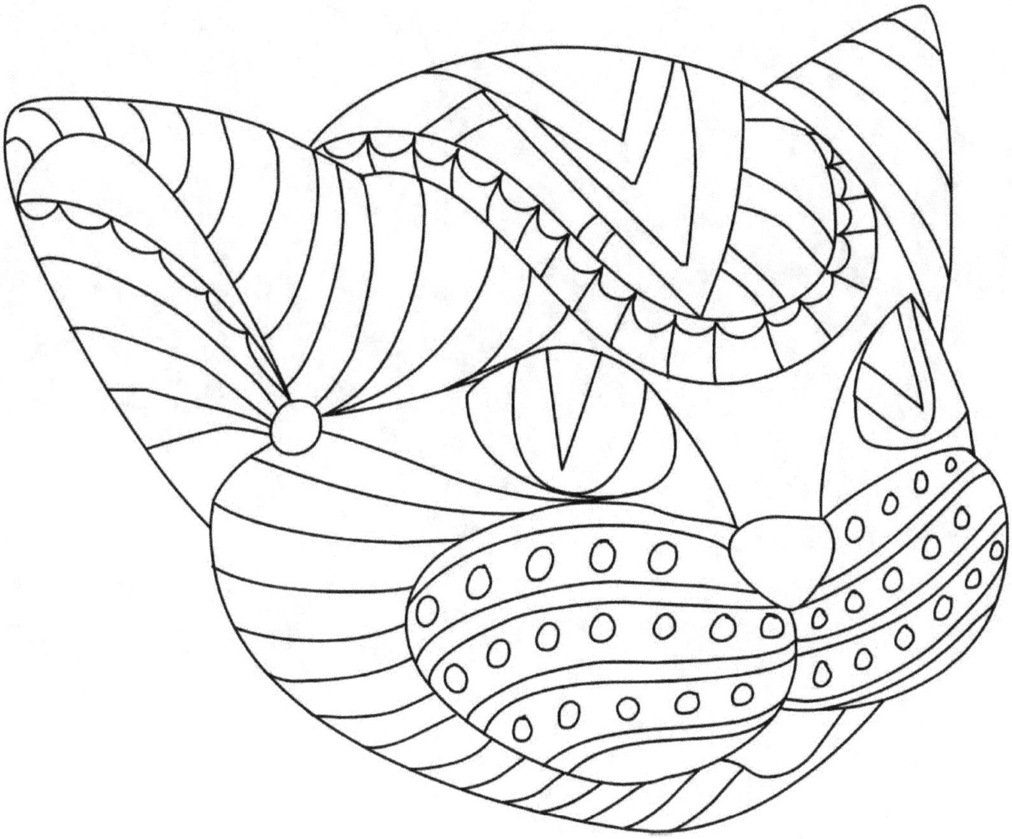

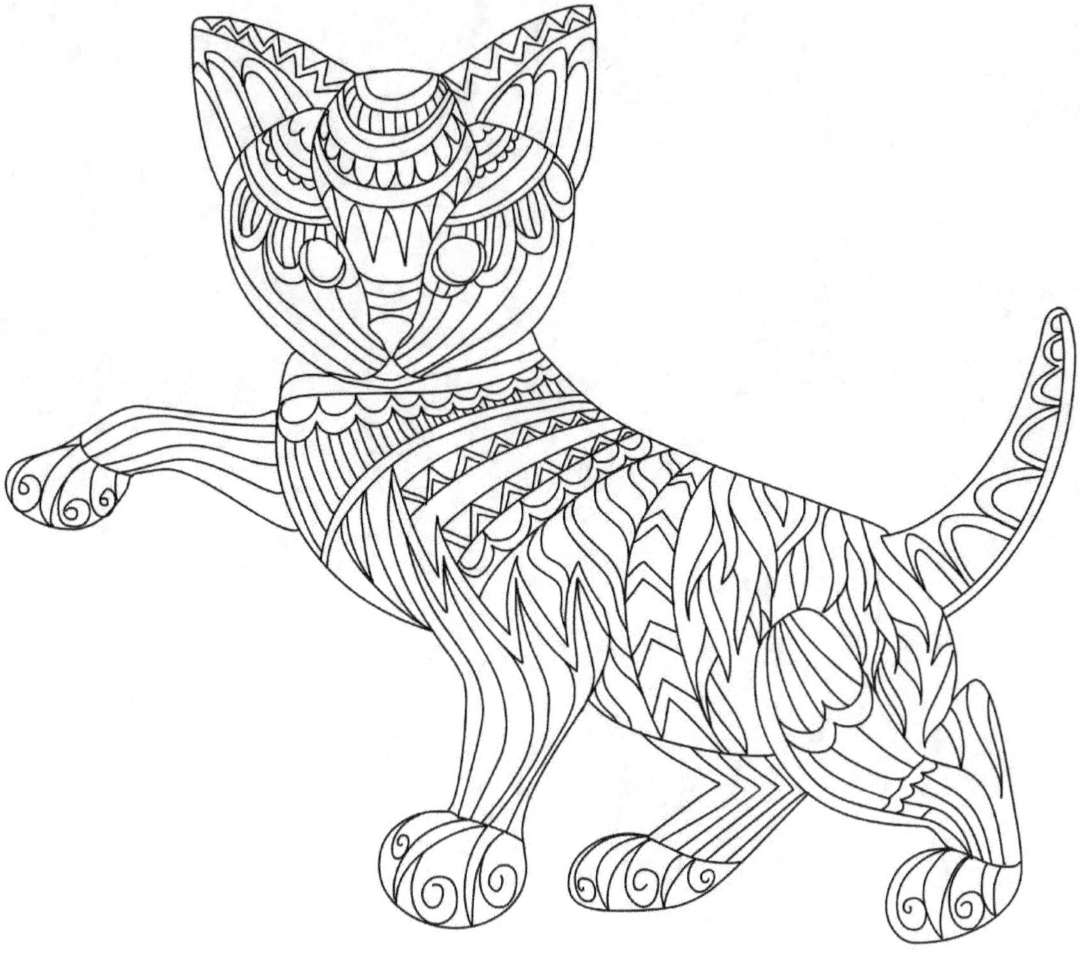

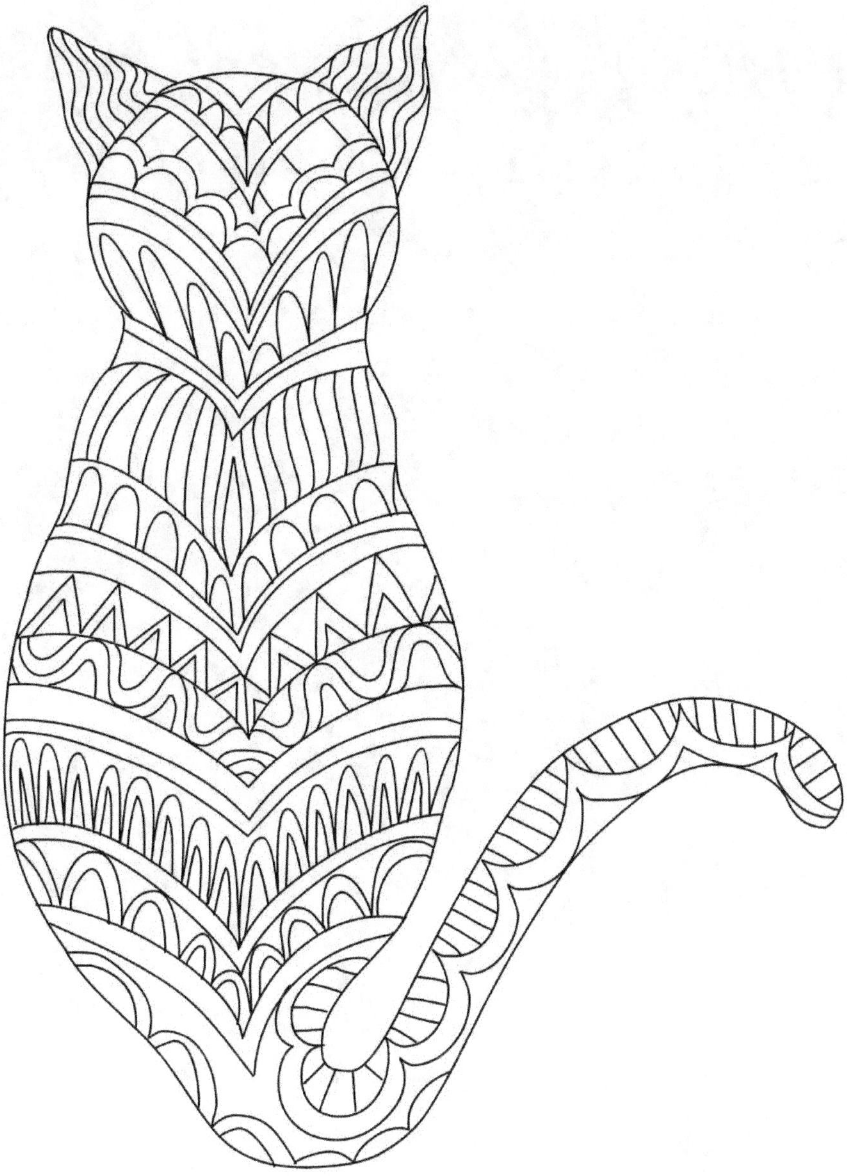

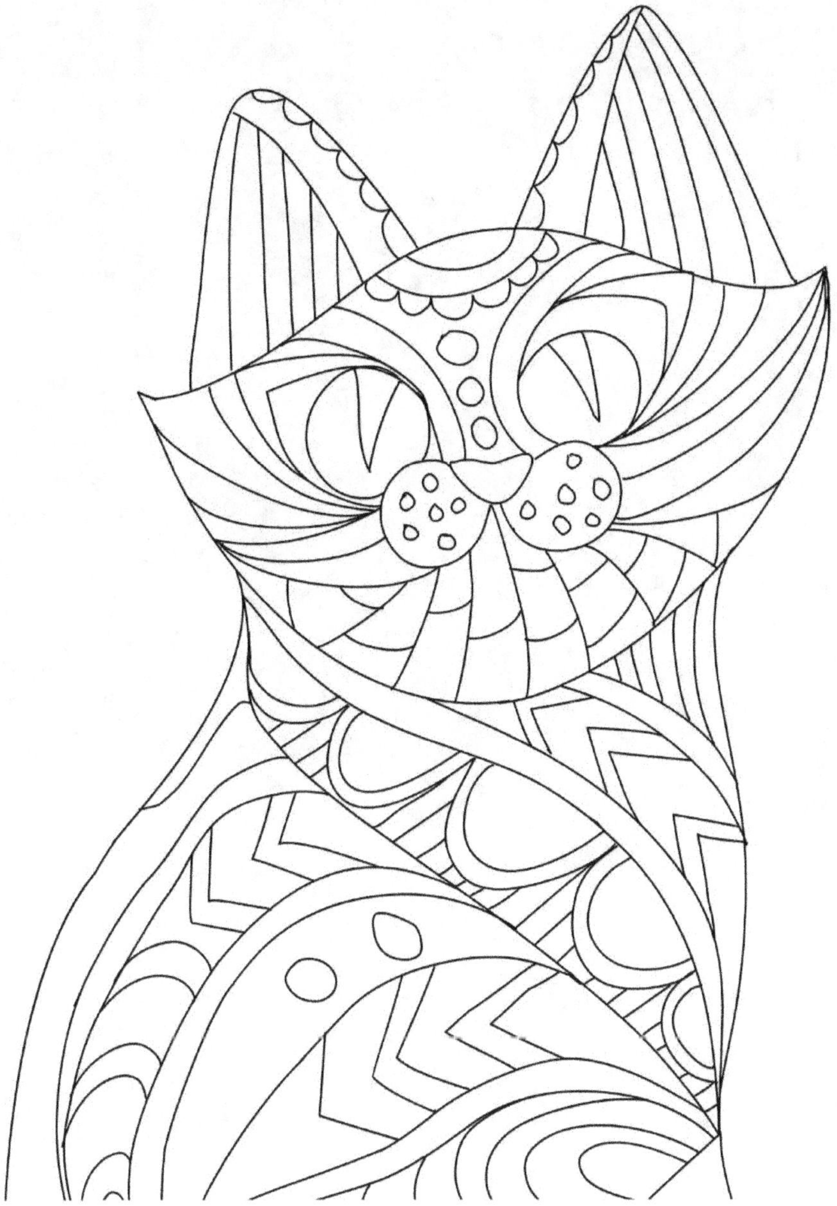

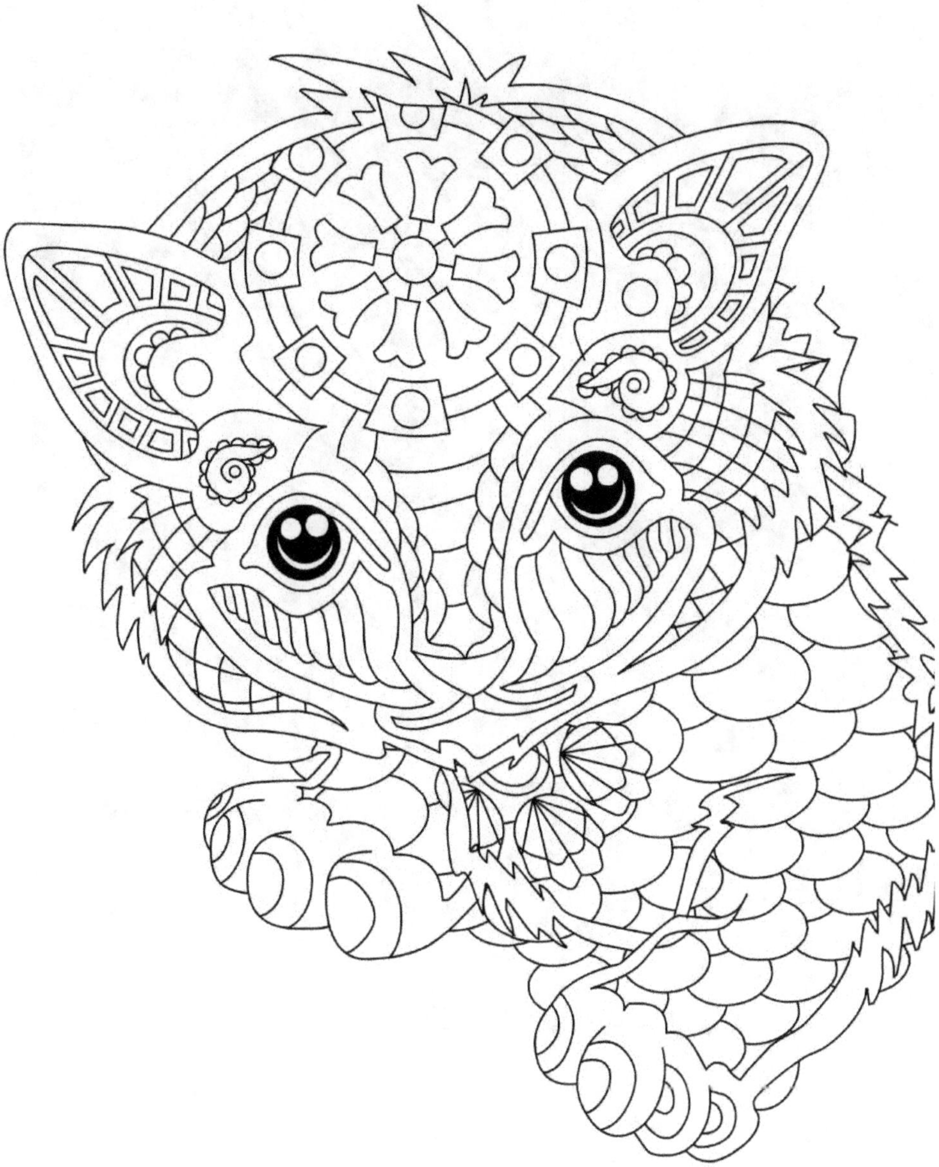

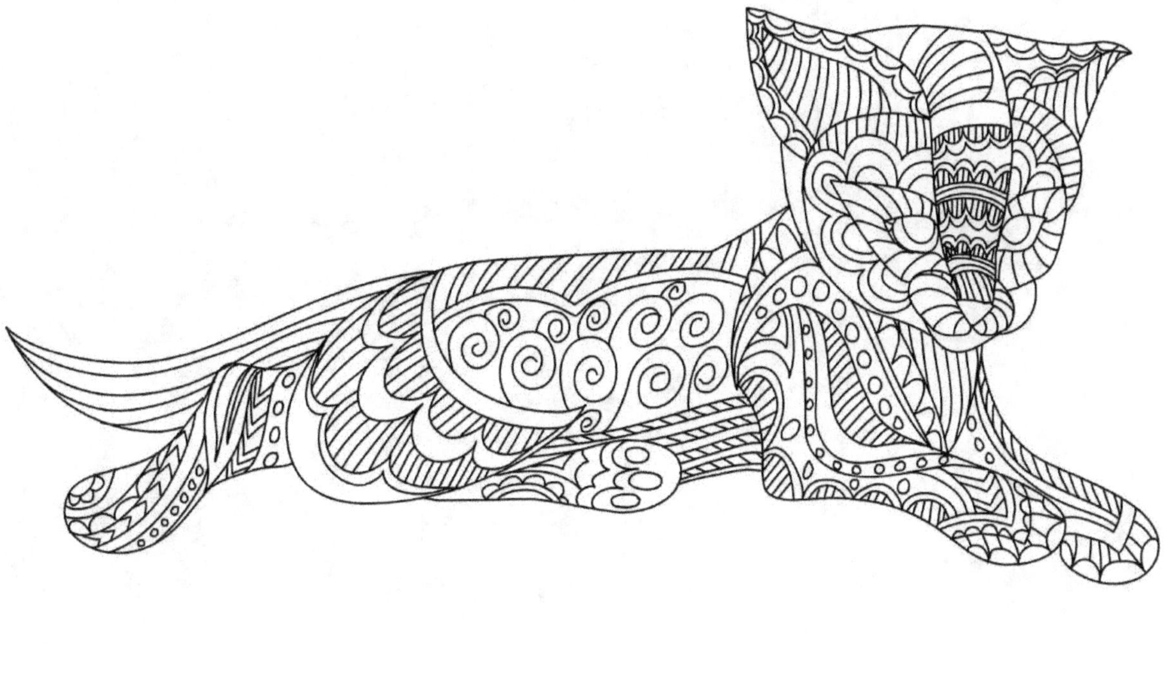

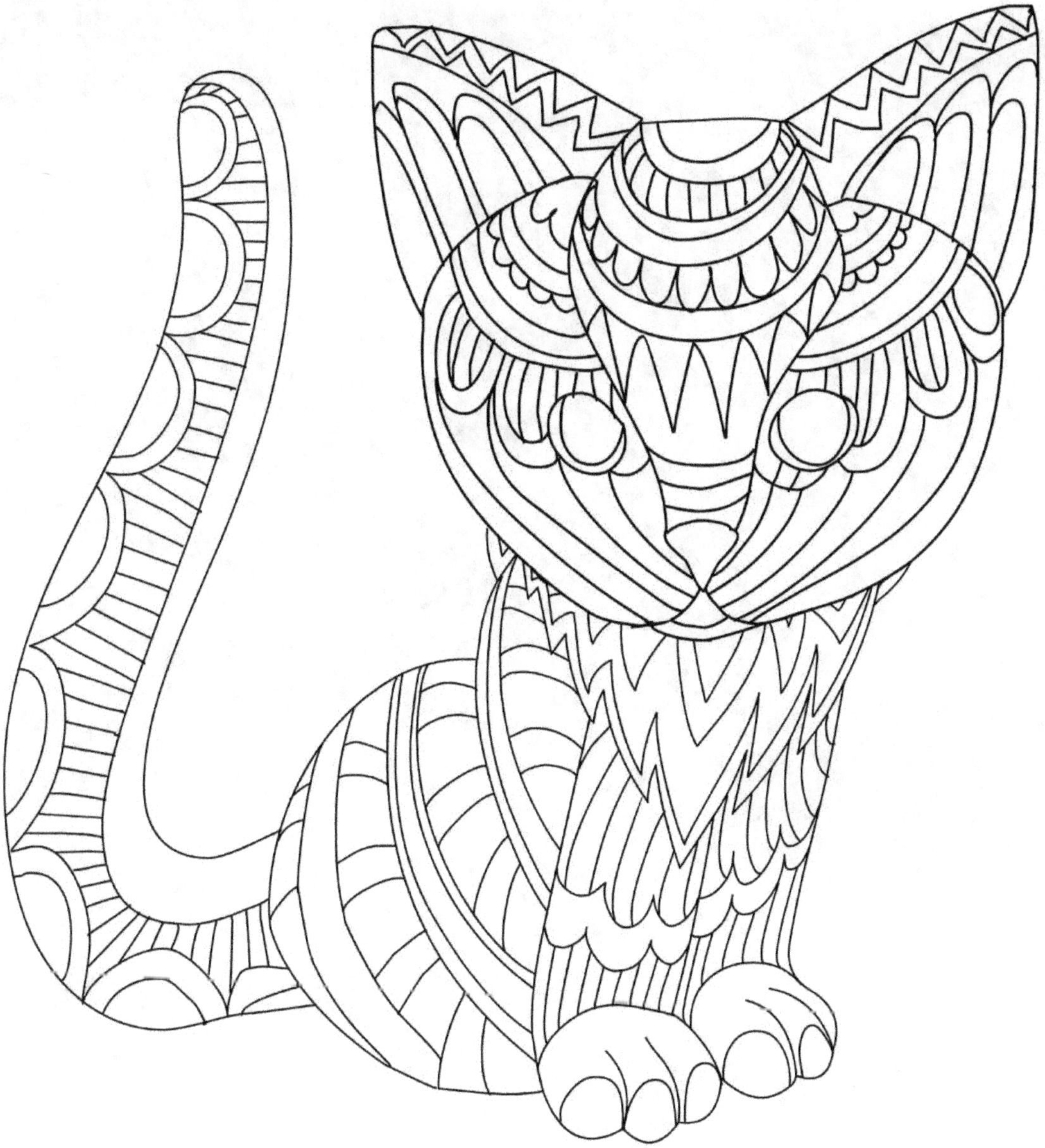

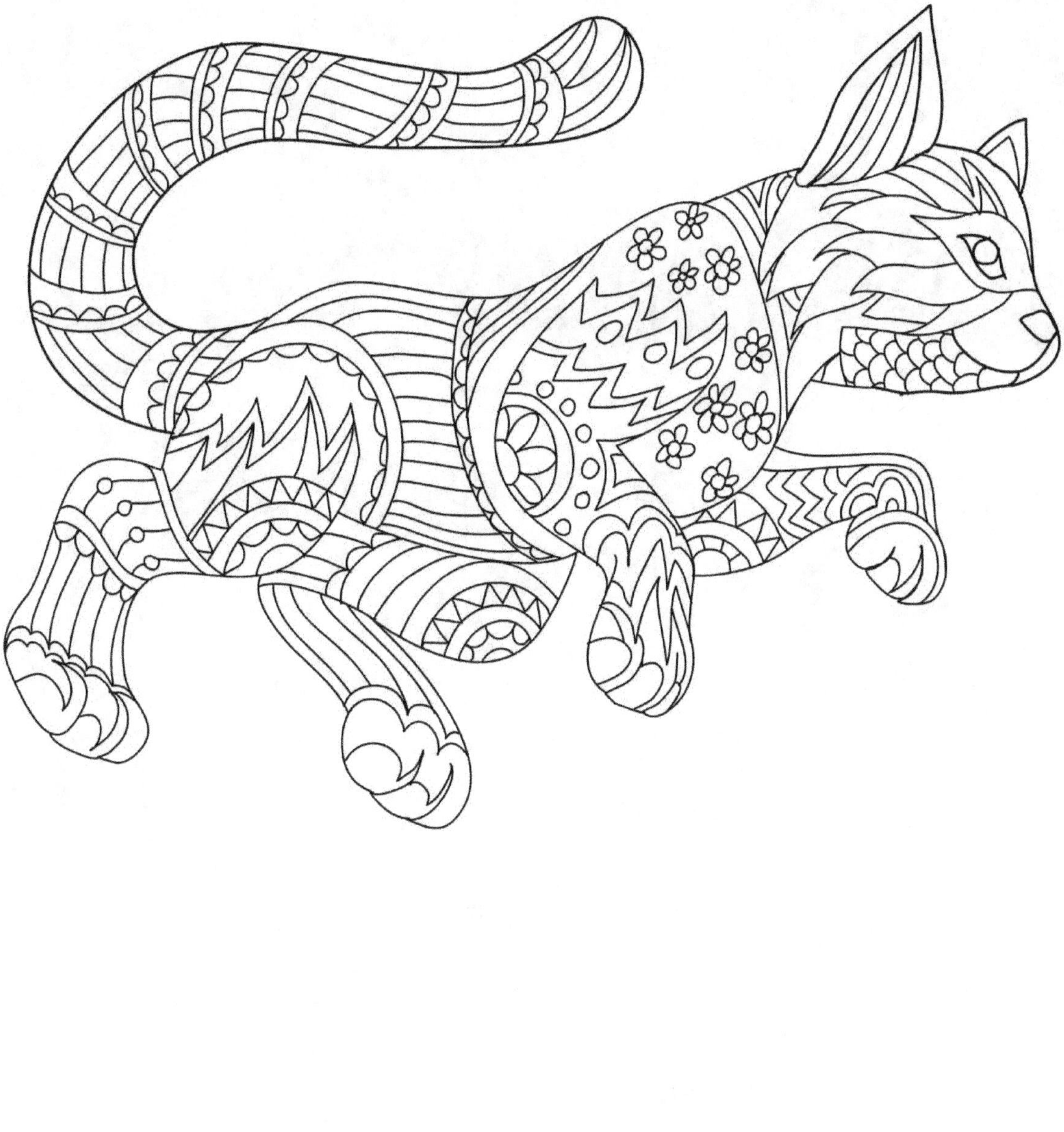

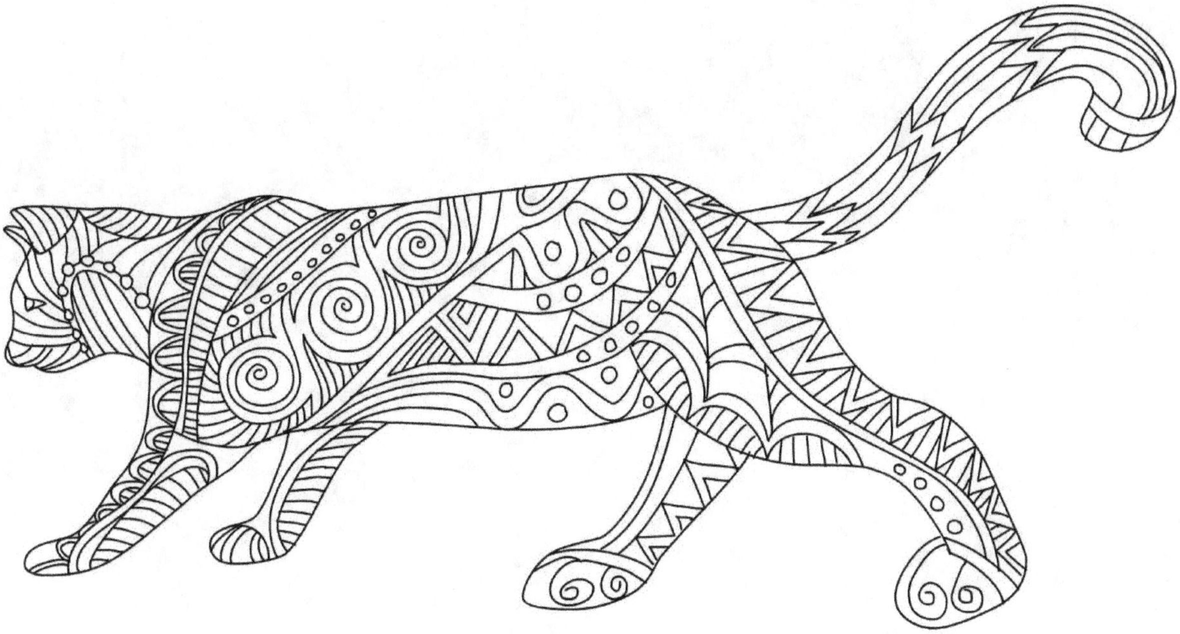

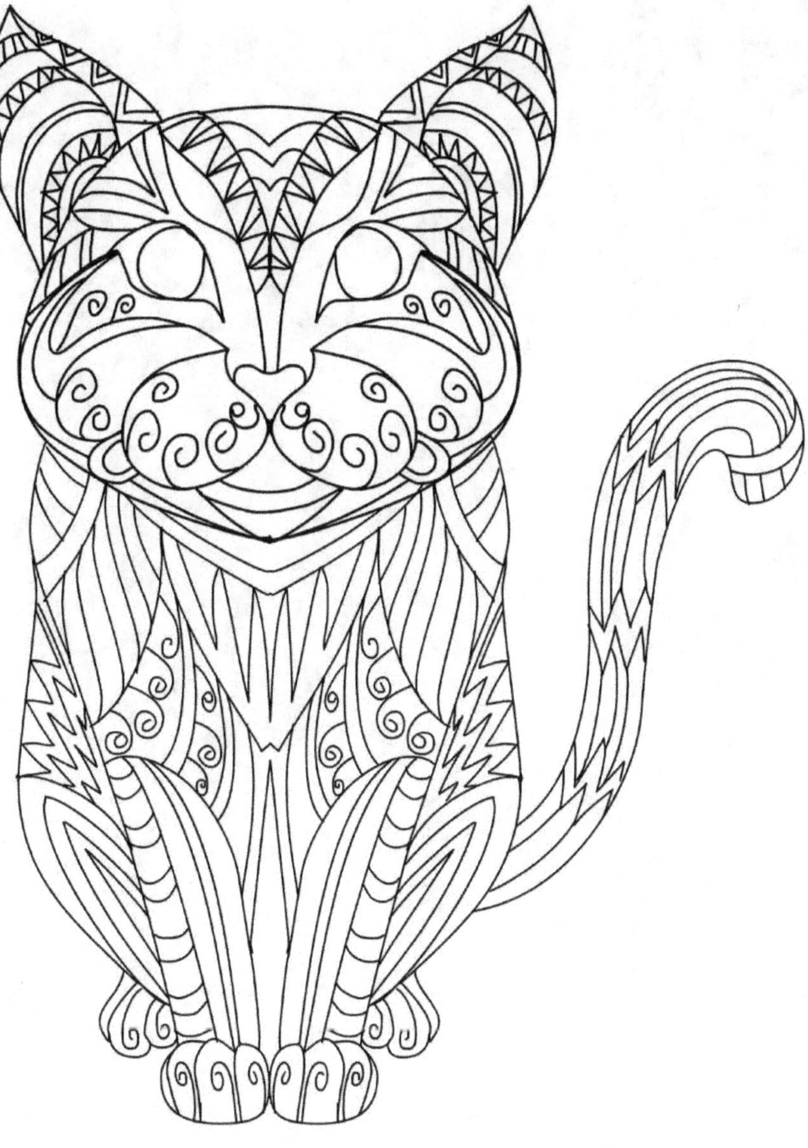

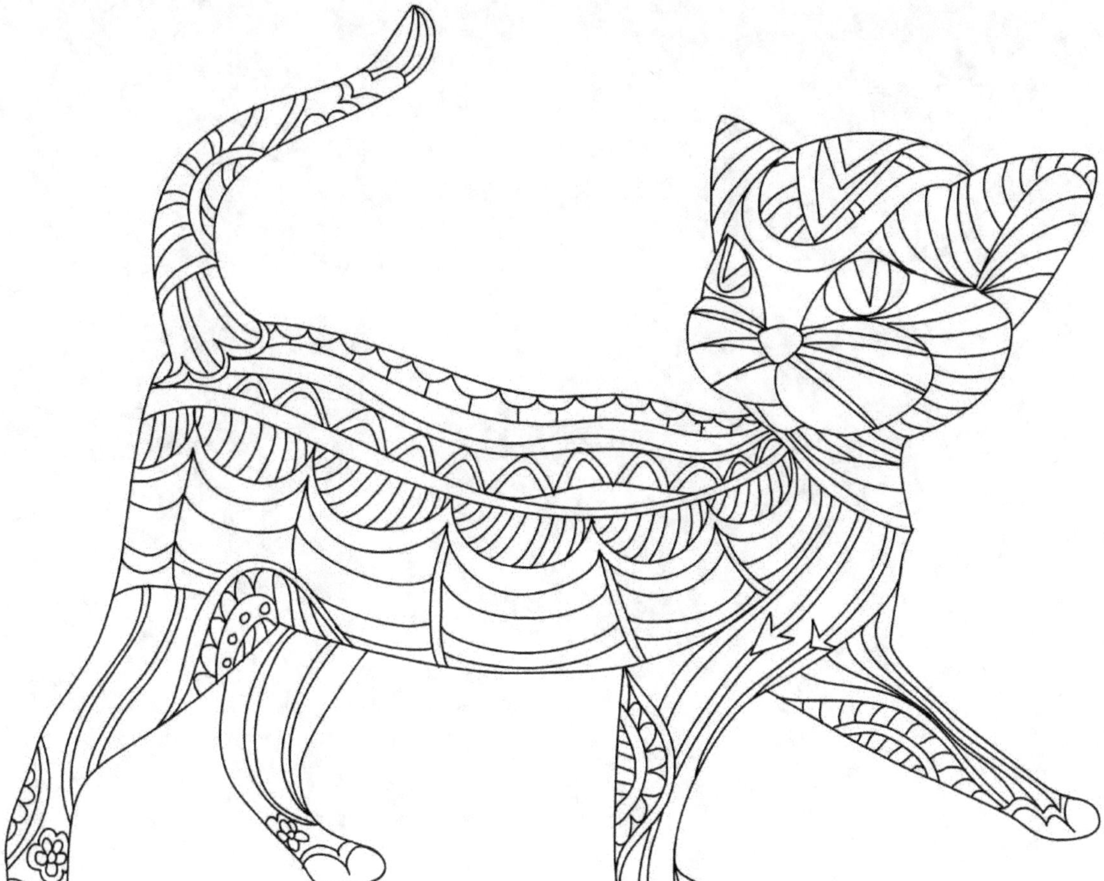

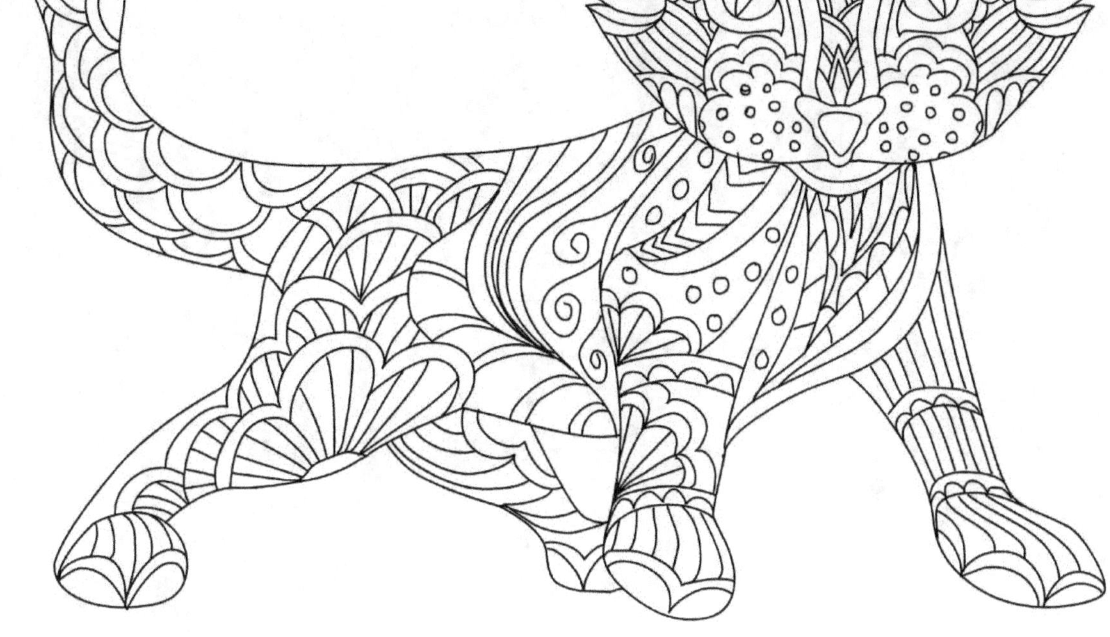

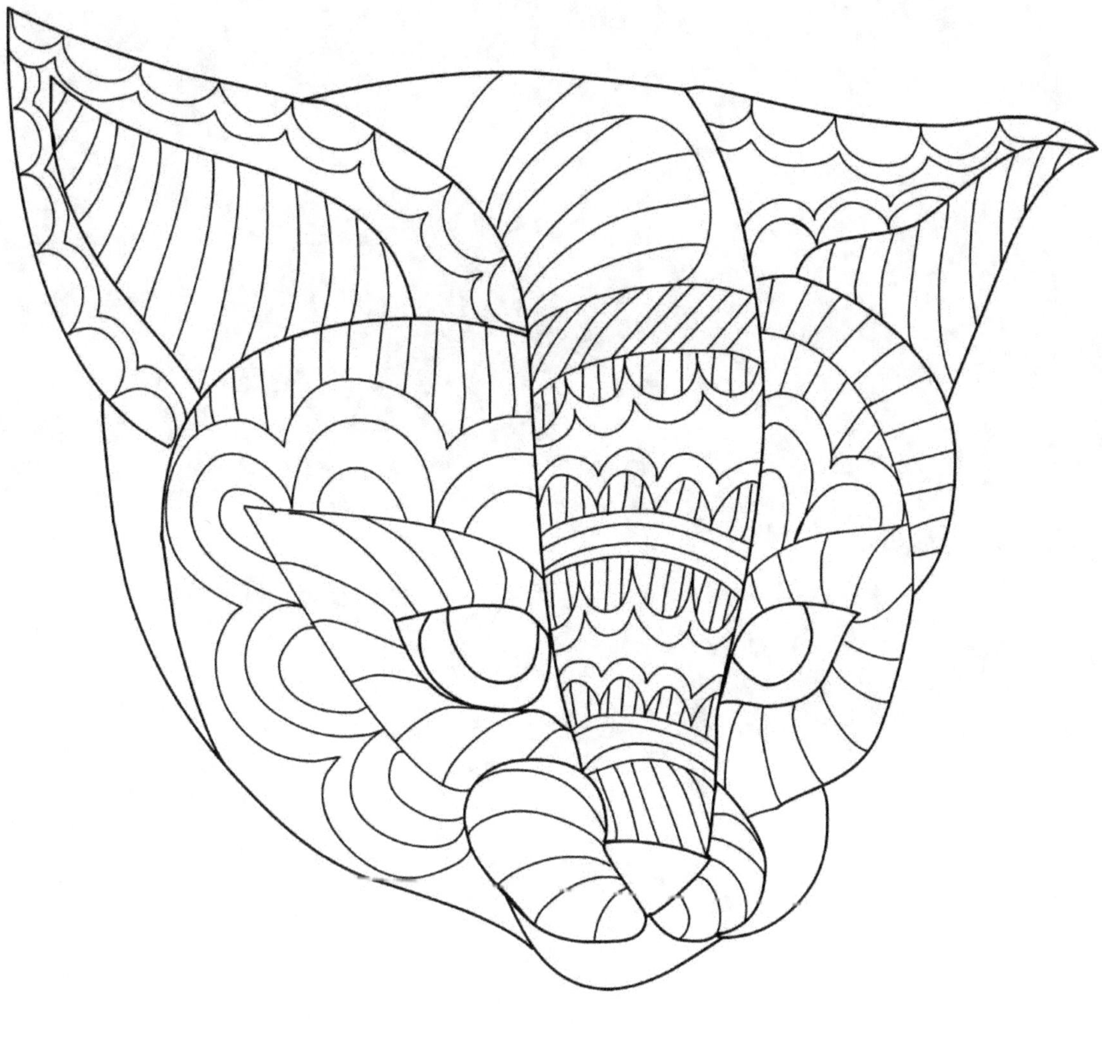

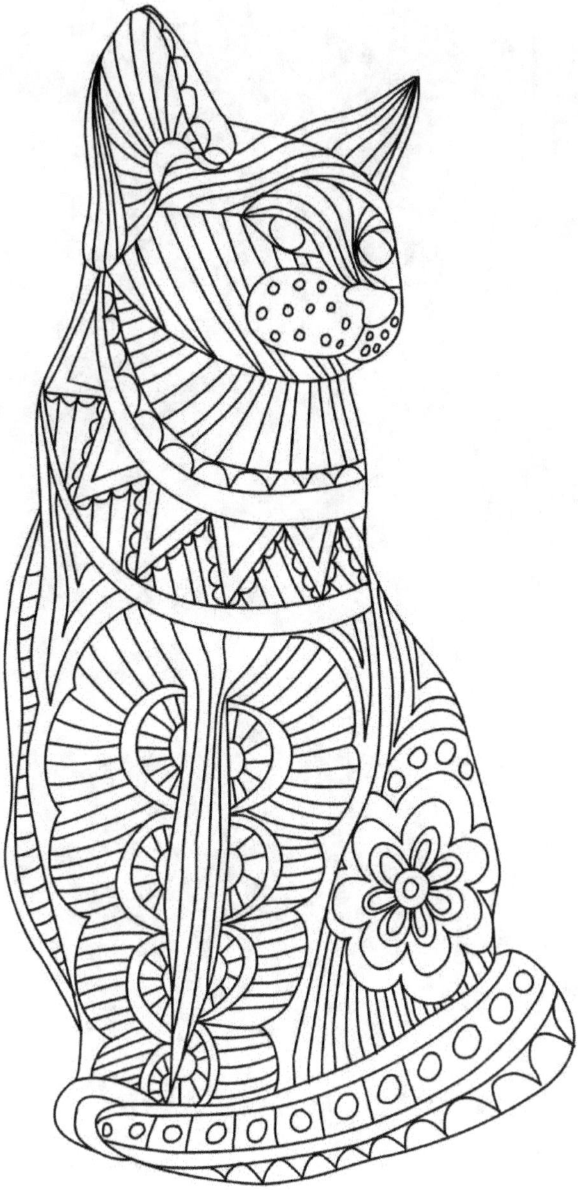

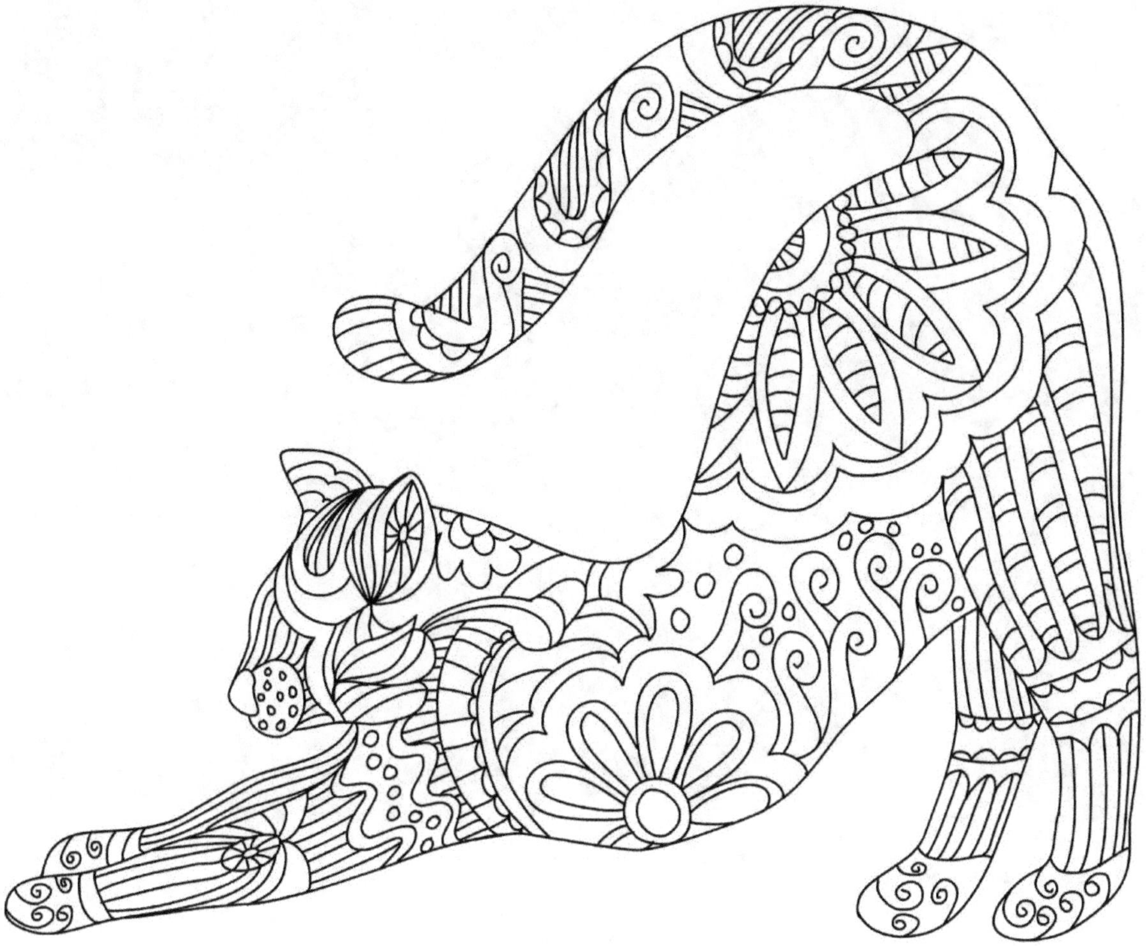

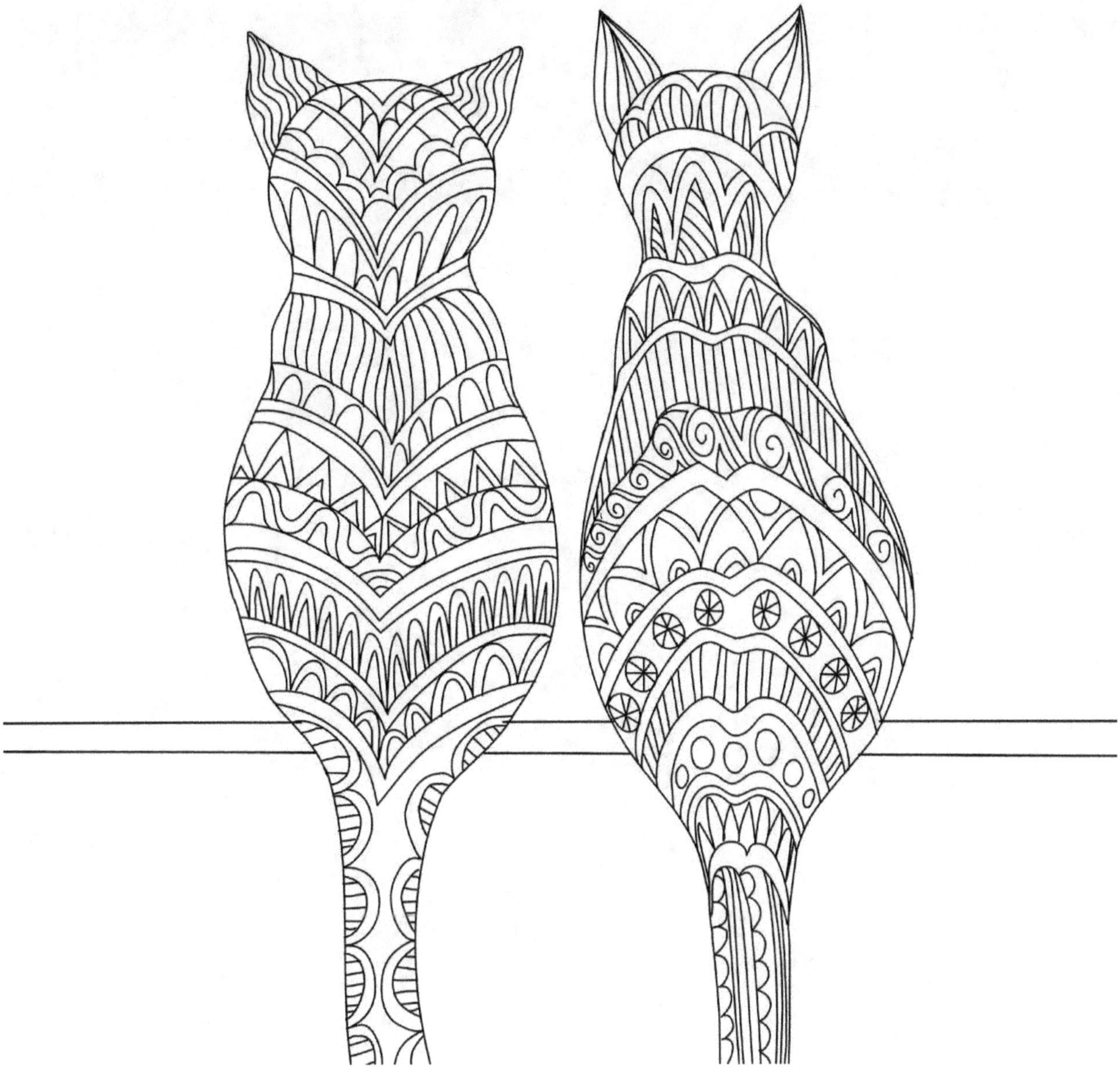

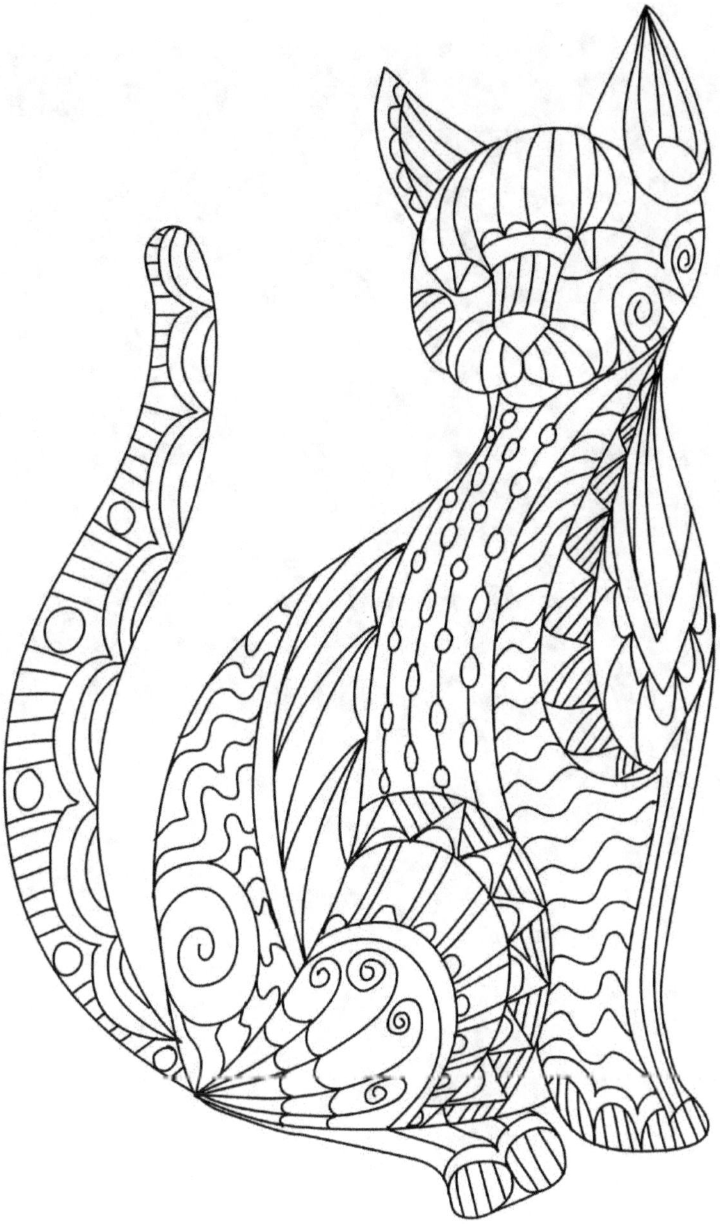

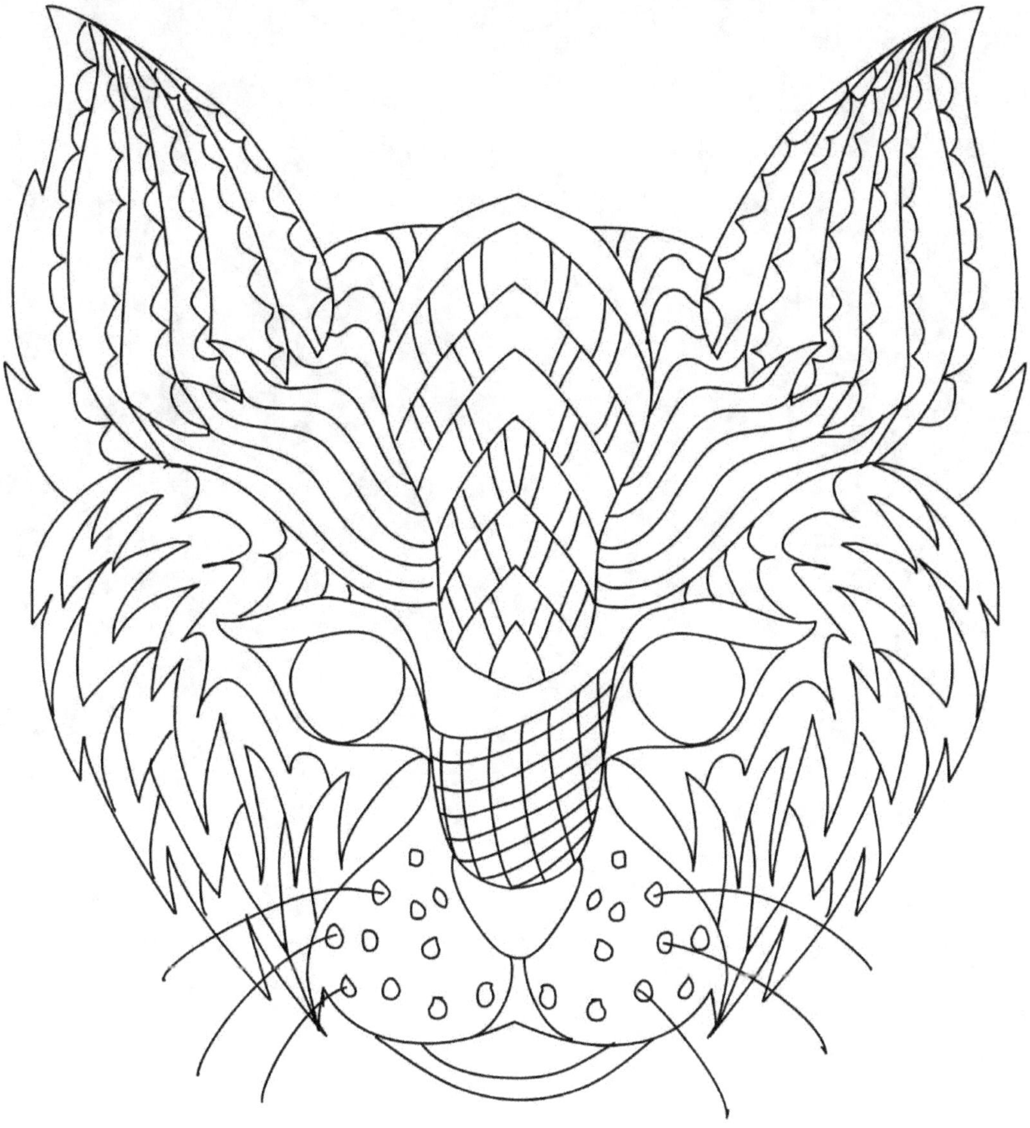

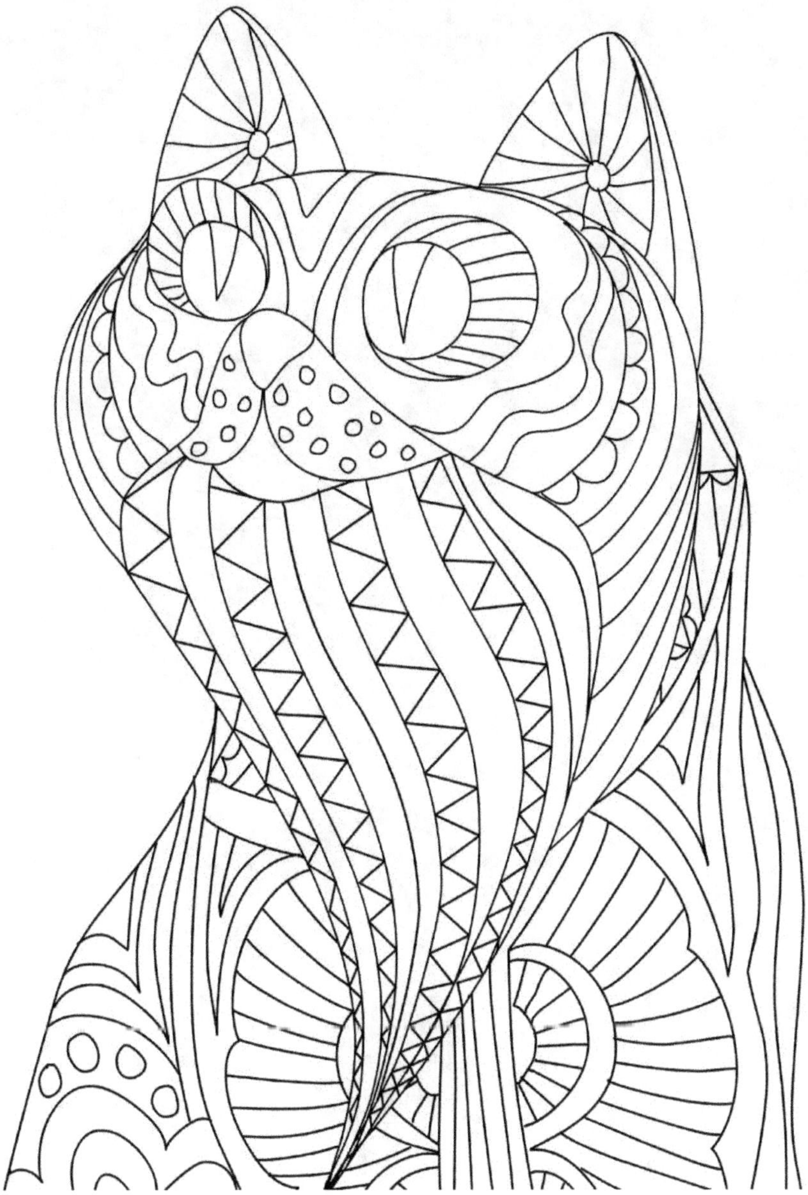

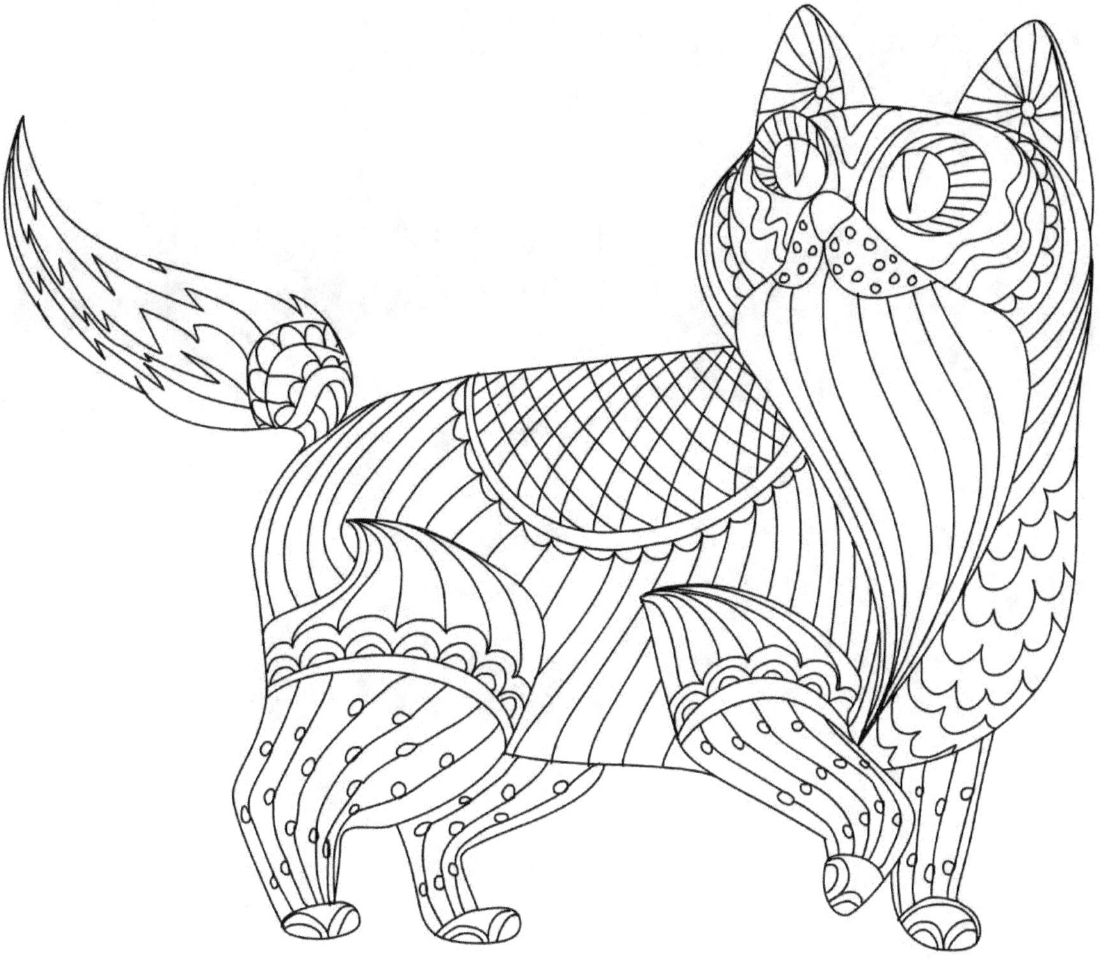

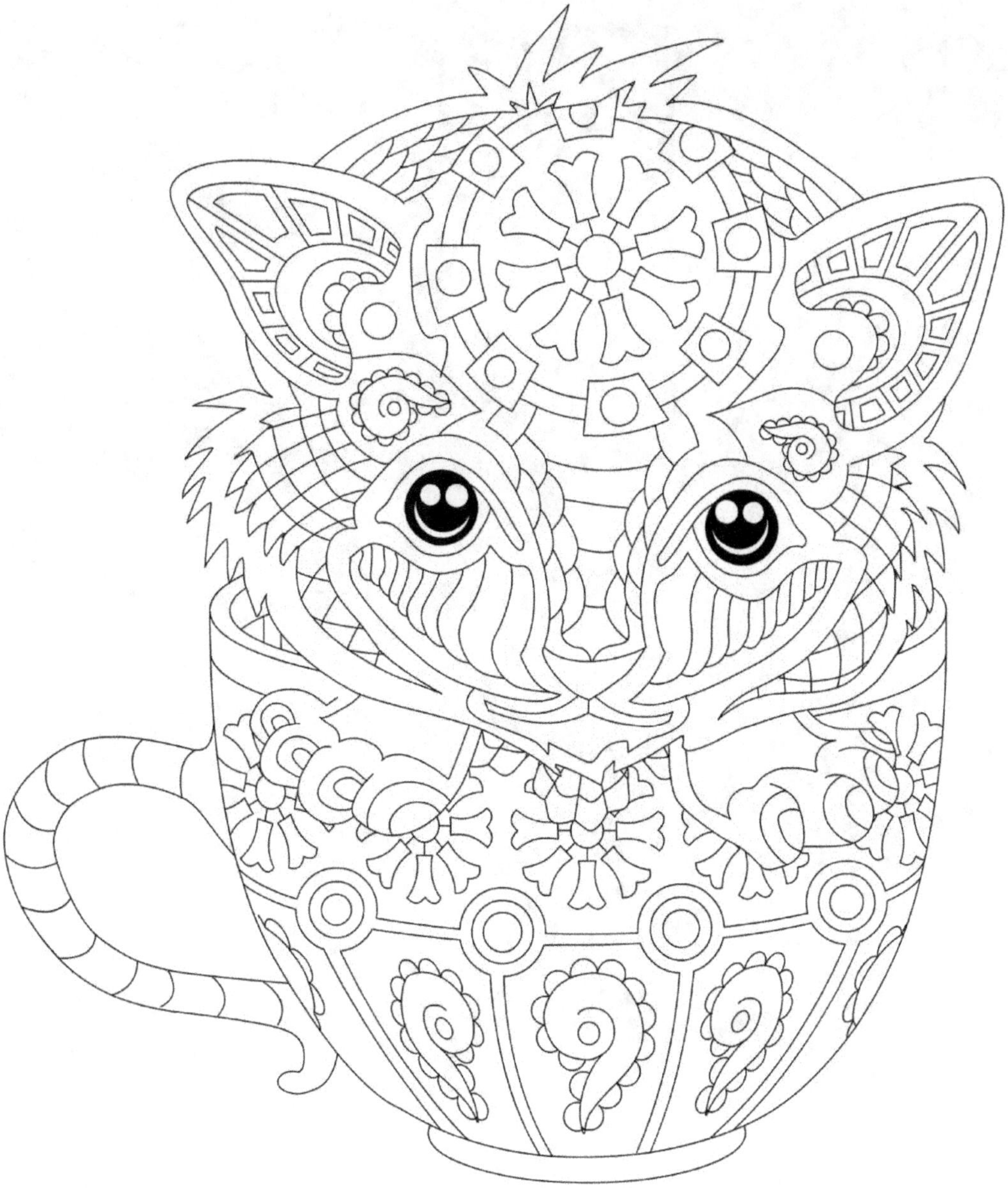

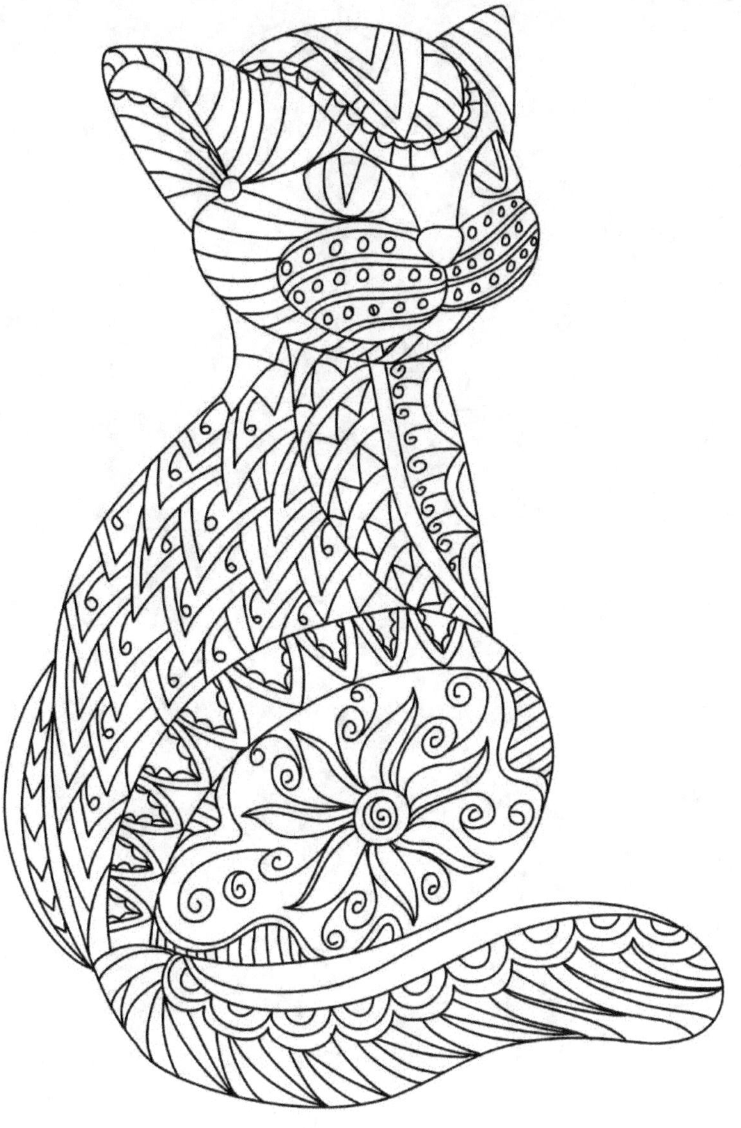

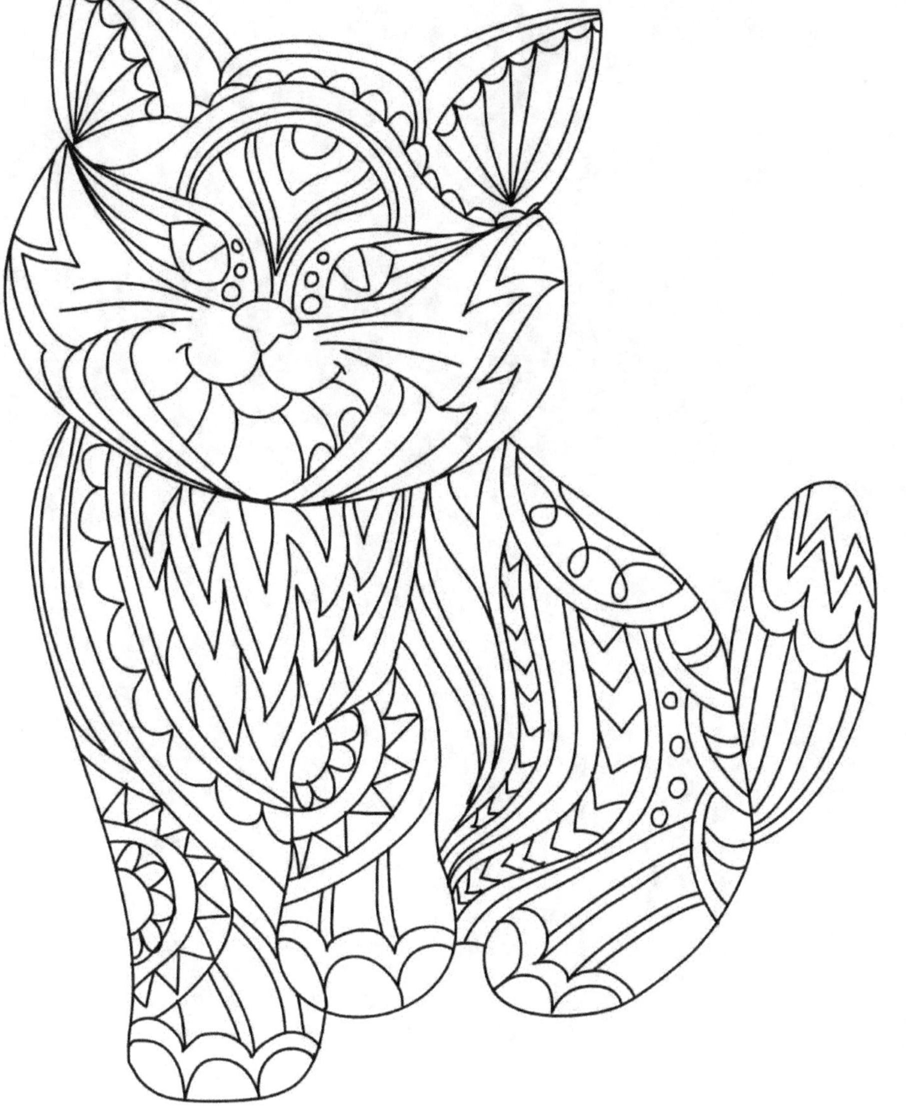

www.ingramcontent.com/pod-product-compliance
Lightning Source LLC
Chambersburg PA
CBHW080923170526
45158CB00008B/2208
* 9 7 8 1 0 7 3 1 1 4 6 4 1 *